Street by Street

WATFORD

BOREHAMWOOD, BUSHEY, RICKMANSWORTH

Abbots Langley, Bricket Wood, Carpenders Park, Chorleywood, Croxley Green, Elstree, Kings Langley, Oxhey, Radlett

CW00666251

1st edition September 2002

© Automobile Association Developments Limited 2002

Ordnance Survey® This product includes map data licensed from Ordnance Survey® with the permission of the Controller of Her Majesty's Stationery Office. © Crown copyright 2002. All rights reserved. Licence No: 399221.

All rights reserved. No part of this publication may be reproduced, stored in a retrieval system, or transmitted in any form or by any means– electronic, mechanical, photocopying, recording or otherwise – unless the permission of the publisher has been given beforehand.

Published by AA Publishing (a trading name of Automobile Association Developments Limited, whose registered office is Millstream, Maidenhead Road, Windsor, Berkshire SL4 5GD. Registered number 1878835).

The Post Office is a registered trademark of Post Office Ltd. in the UK and other countries.
.
Schools address data provided by Education Direct.

One-way street data provided by:

Tele Atlas   © Tele Atlas N.V.

Mapping produced by the Cartographic Department of The Automobile Association. A01100

A CIP Catalogue record for this book is available from the British Library.

Printed by GRAFIASA S.A., Porto, Portugal

The contents of this atlas are believed to be correct at the time of the latest revision. However, the publishers cannot be held responsible for loss occasioned to any person acting or refraining from action as a result of any material in this atlas, nor for any errors, omissions or changes in such material. This does not affect your statutory rights. The publishers would welcome information to correct any errors or omissions and to keep this atlas up to date. Please write to Publishing, The Automobile Association, Fanum House (FH17), Basing View, Basingstoke, Hampshire, RG21 4EA.

Ref: ML188

Key to map pages	ii-iii
Key to map symbols	iv-1
Enlarged scale pages	2-3
Street by Street	4-35
Index – towns & villages	36
Index – streets	37-43
Index – featured places	43-44

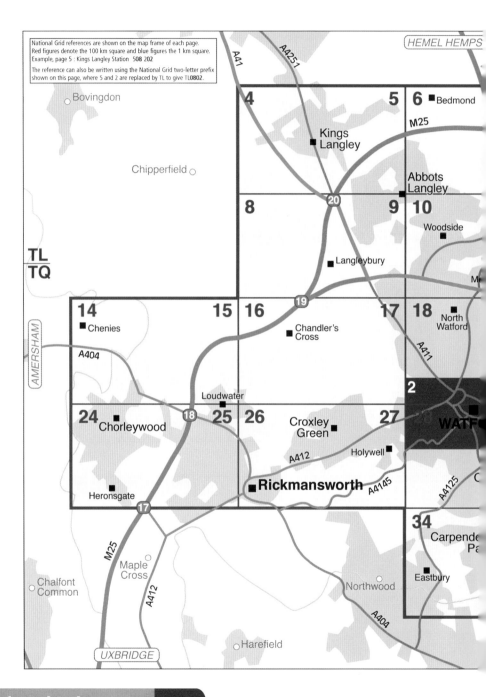

ii

National Grid references are shown on the map frame of each page.
Red figures denote the 100 km square and blue figures the 1 km square.
Example, page 5 : Kings Langley Station **508 202**

The reference can also be written using the National Grid two-letter prefix
shown on this page, where 5 and 2 are replaced by TL to give TL**0802**.

HEMEL HEMPS

Bovingdon

Chipperfield

4

5

6 ■ Bedmond

M25

Kings
Langley ■

Abbots
Langley

8

20

9 **10**

Woodside ■

TL
TQ

Langleybury ■

19

14

15 **16**

17 **18**

North
Watford ■

■ Chenies

Chandler's
Cross ■

A404

AMERSHAM

A411

Loudwater ■

2

24

25 **26**

Croxley
Green ■

27

WATF

Chorleywood ■

18

A412

Holywell ■

Heronsgate ■

Rickmansworth ■

A4145

A4125

17

34

M25

Maple
Cross

Carpend
Pa

A412

Northwood

Eastbury ■

Chalfont
Common

A404

Harefield

UXBRIDGE

Enlarged scale pages **1:10,000** 6.3 inches to 1 mile

| 0 | 1/4 | miles | 1/2 |
| 0 | 1/4 | 1/2 kilometres | 3/4 | 1 |

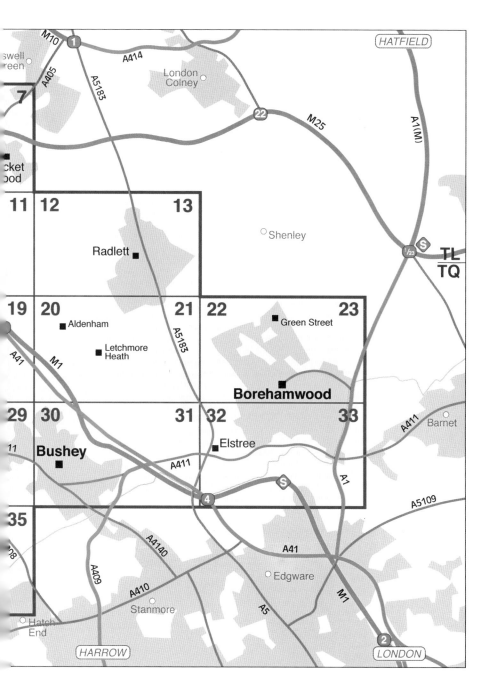

swell
reen

M10

A414

A405

A5183

London
Colney

7

cket
ood

A11(M)

M25

22

11 | **12** | **13**

Radlett

Shenley

1/23 S

TL
TQ

19 | **20** | **21** | **22** | **23**

Aldenham

Green Street

A41

M1

A5183

Letchmore
Heath

Borehamwood

29 | **30** | **31** | **32** | **33**

11

Bushey

Elstree

A411

A411

Barnet

A1

4

S

A5109

35

08

A4140

A41

A409

Edgware

M1

A410

A5

Stanmore

Hatch
End

HARROW

LONDON

2

4.2 inches to I mile **Scale of main map pages 1:15,000**

0 | 1/4 | miles | 1/2 | 3/4 | 1

iv

Junction 9	Motorway & junction
Services	Motorway service area
	Primary road single/dual carriageway
Services	Primary road service area
	A road single/dual carriageway
	B road single/dual carriageway
	Other road single/dual carriageway
	Minor/private road, access may be restricted
← ←	One-way street
	Pedestrian area
	Track or footpath
	Road under construction
	Road tunnel
AA	AA Service Centre
P	Parking
P+	Park & Ride
	Bus/coach station
	Railway & main railway station
	Railway & minor railway station

⊖	Underground station
⊖	Light railway & station
+++++++	Preserved private railway
LC	Level crossing
●—●—●—●	Tramway
- - - - -	Ferry route
....	Airport runway
— · — · —	County, administrative boundary
ⅣⅣⅣⅣ	Mounds
17	Page continuation 1:15,000
3	Page continuation to enlarged scale 1:10,000
	River/canal, lake, pier
	Aqueduct, lock, weir
465 ▲ Winter Hill	Peak (with height in metres)
	Beach
	Woodland
	Park
	Cemetery
	Built-up area

	Featured building		Abbey, cathedral or priory
	City wall		Castle
A&E	Hospital with 24-hour A&E department		Historic house or building
PO	Post Office	Wakehurst Place NT	National Trust property
	Public library	M	Museum or art gallery
i	Tourist Information Centre		Roman antiquity
	Petrol station Major suppliers only		Ancient site, battlefield or monument
†	Church/chapel		Industrial interest
	Public toilets		Garden
	Toilet with disabled facilities		Arboretum
PH	Public house AA recommended		Farm or animal centre
	Restaurant AA inspected		Zoological or wildlife collection
	Theatre or performing arts centre		Bird collection
	Cinema		Nature reserve
	Golf course	V	Visitor or heritage centre
▲	Camping AA inspected		Country park
	Caravan Site AA inspected		Cave
	Camping & caravan site AA inspected		Windmill
	Theme park		Distillery, brewery or vineyard

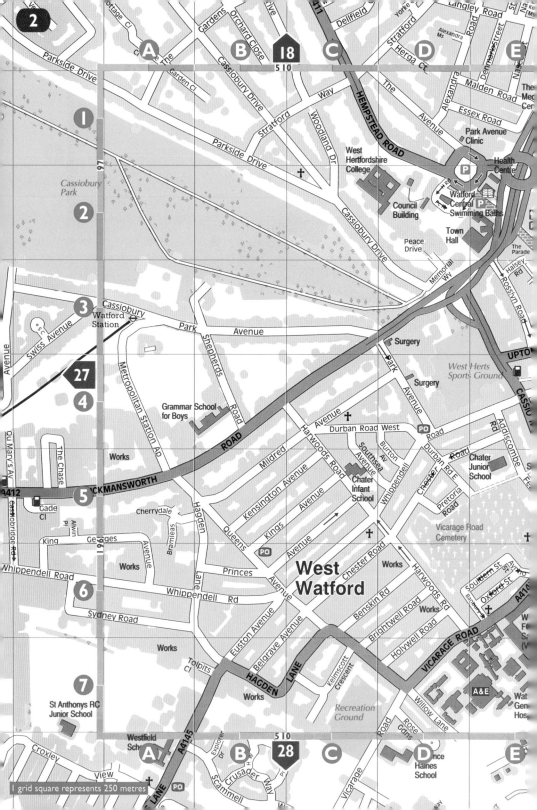

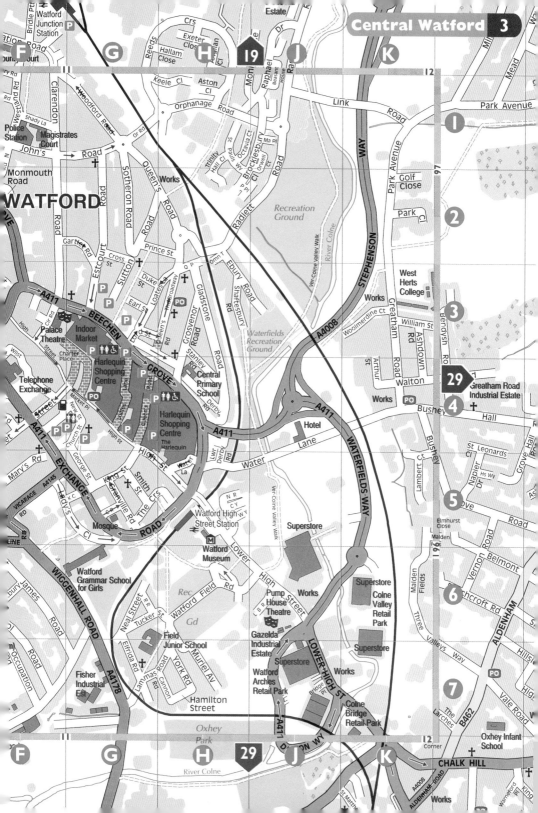

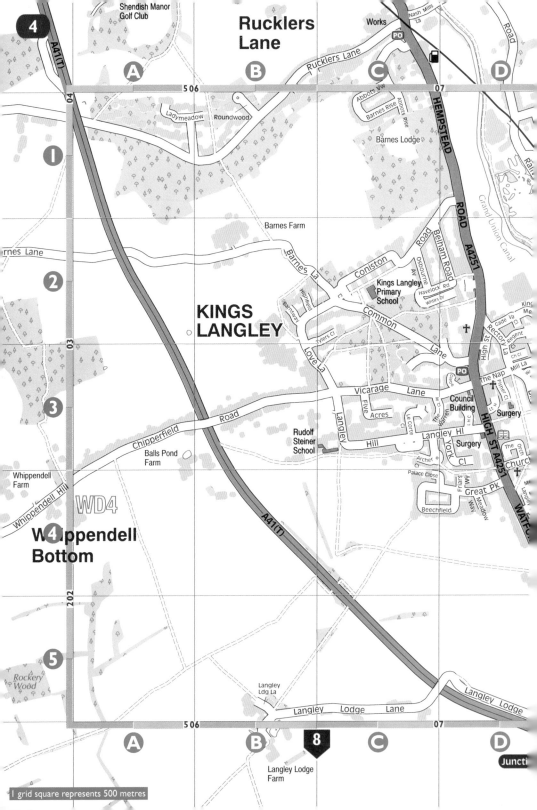

Shendish Manor
Golf Club

**Rucklers
Lane**

Works

Nash Mills
La

Road

Road

PO

Ⓐ 5 06 Ⓑ Rucklers Lane Ⓒ 07 Ⓓ

Abbots VW

Barnes Rise

Abbots Rise

HEMPSTEAD

Ladymeadow Roundwood

Barnes Lodge

Ⓘ

Rail

Grand Union Canal

Barnes Farm

ROAD

A4251

Road

Belham Road

Osbourne
Av

Coniston

rnes Lane

Barnes La

Kings Langley
Primary
School

Havelock Rd

whtfrs br

Ⓞ

Highfield

Barnsway

**KINGS
LANGLEY**

Common

Love La

Tylers Cl

Lane

High St

Cade Va

Rectory La

regent

King
Me

Ch Cl

Ⓙ

PO

Ⓒ

Glene

Mill La
W

Ⓧ

Vicarage

Lane

Council
Building

The Nap

Fisher Cl

Ⓧ

H

Chipperfield

Road

Five
Acres

Langley

Le Corte
Cl

Warren

Surgery

Ⓦ

Balls Pond
Farm

Rudolf
Steiner
School

Hill

Langley HI

York
Cl

Surgery

The
Orch

Church

Ⓧ

Whippendell
Farm

Archet
Cl

Palace Close

Friars
Cl

WATF.

WD4

A41(T)

Beechfield

Great PK

Meadow
Way

Lanes

M

Whippendell Hill

**W4ippendell
Bottom**

202

Ⓢ

Rockery
Wood

Ⓐ 5 06 Ⓑ Langley Ldg La Langley Lodge Lane 07 Ⓒ Langley Lodge Ⓓ

8

Juncti

Langley Lodge
Farm

6

A B C D

Hart Hall Farm

Sergehill

Whitehouse Farm

Lane

Bedmond Lane

St. Albans Lane

Lane

Whitehouse Lane

Sea

Bedmond

Church Hl

High St

Bluebell Dr

PO

Millhouse Lane

Millhouse Farm

searches

Searches Farm

I

Henderson Wy

Meadow Wy

Tom's Lane

Bell Lane

Bell Cl

Bedmond JMI School

2

Sheppey's La

Tenements Farm

East Lane

Bedmond Road

M25

3

5

Dairy Wy

Abbots Langley Primary School

Love La

East Lane

Chequers Lane

Parsonage

Tibbs Hl Rd

Summerhouse Wy

Summerhouse Wy

Cem

Cem

East Lane

Waterda

4

St Lawrence Cl

High St

Breakspear Cl

The Crs

Tibbs Hl Rd

Jacketts Fld

Works

Woodside Road

High Elms Lane

Parmi Scho

Abbots Road

PO

Langley Road

Adrian Road

Hill Lane

Surgery

Council Building

Greasy Cl

Tibbs Hill Road

Jacketts Field

Ngn Rd

Rdwn Cr

Mallard Cl

Linnet Road

5

Breakspeare Road

Rise

Tylersfield

College Road

Harlech Rd

Harlech Road

Chequers Lane

Trowley

Follett Dr

Cherry Hollow

Wadham Ln Wy

Marlin Sq

Tanners Hl

Ldwn Wy

Stewart Cl

Leavesden Hospital

Abbotswood Medical

10

Boundary Wy

Boundary Wy

Oak Gn

Keble Ter

Furtherfield

Haviland Wy

Queens Road

Edward Cl

Mrgrt Cl

Helps Rd

Shires Road

Pryor Cl

Magnolia Av

Hawthorn Cl

Arundell Road

Balmoral Rd

Cardiff Wy

Stirling Wy

Whitley Wy

Kenilworth Close

Blackthorn Close

Grasmere Wy

Seshoe

Louvain Wy

Poplars Wy

Francis

A B C D

1 grid square represents 500 metres

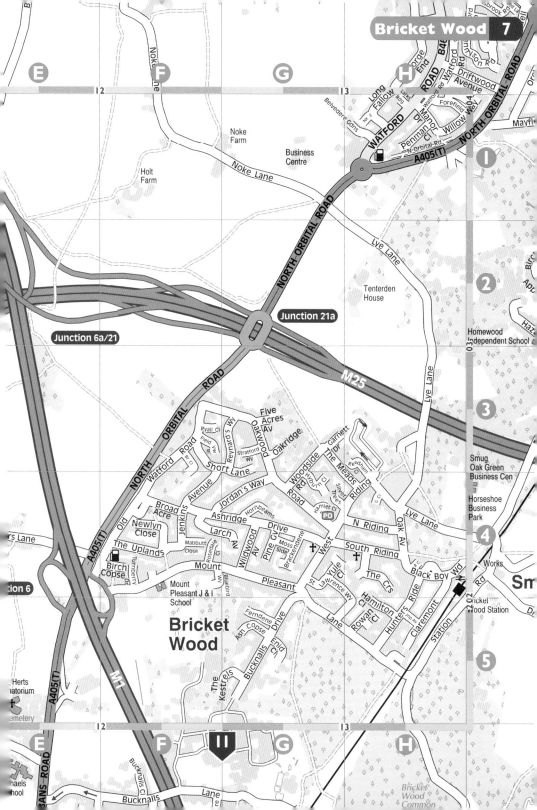

E F G H

12 13

I

Noke Lane

Noke Farm

Holt Farm

Business Centre

Belvedere Gdns

Long Fallow

WATFORD

N-Orbital-Rd

Penman Cl

Manor Cl

Forefield

Driftwood Avenue

Willow Way

ROAD B4

NORTH ORBITAL ROAD

A405(T)

Mayfl

NORTH ORBITAL ROAD

Lye Lane

Tenterden House

2

Homewood Independent School

Junction 21a

Junction 6a/21

M25

Lye Lane

3

Smug Oak Green Business Cen

Horseshoe Business Park

Five Acres Av

Oakridge

Garnett Dr

The Meads

Riding

Woodside Rd

Oakwood

Reynard's Wy

Stratford Wy

Ryall Cl

Field Vw

Short Lane

Watford Road

Avenue

NORTH

ORBITAL

ROAD

Jordan's Way

Hornbeams

Ashridge

Broad Acre

Jenkins

Newlyn Close

The Uplands

Birch Copse

Turnberry

Old

A405(T)

tion 6

A405(T)

M1

Larch AV

Mabbutt Close

Wildwood AV

Rosedale

Mount

Pine

Gv

Moss Side

Brackendene

Drive

Pleasant

Bluebird Wy

Mount Pleasant J & I School

Bricket Wood

Ferndene

Ash Copse

Bucknalls

Enid

Drive

The Kestrels

Lye Lane

Oak Av

N Riding

West

South Riding

Yule Cl

St Lawrence Wy

Hamilton Cl

Rowan Cl

Hunter's Ride

The Crs

Black Boy

Claremont

Station Rd

Works

Sm

Bricket Wood Station

4

5

Woodside Rd

Hamlet Cl

Silver Trees

PO

Garnett Dr

Reedham

Lane

Herts matorium

Cemetery

E F G H

12 13

Bucknalls Cl

Bucknalls Lane

Bricket Wood Common

8

Rockery Wood

A 5 06 **B** Langley dg La **4** La Lodge Lane **C** Langle **D** Langle dge La

Junctio

1 10

Langley Lodge Farm

2 Jeffery's Farm

Berrybushes Wood

Baytree Farm

Model Farm

Bucks Hill

3 200

Bucks Hill

Great Westwood

4 Old House Lane

Bottom Lane

Buck's Hill Bottom

5 1 99

Newhall Farm

Tom's Hill

Junction 1

5 06 **B** Templep Yew Co Farm **16** Lane **C** M25 **D**

A

White House

Chandle

1 grid square represents 500 metres

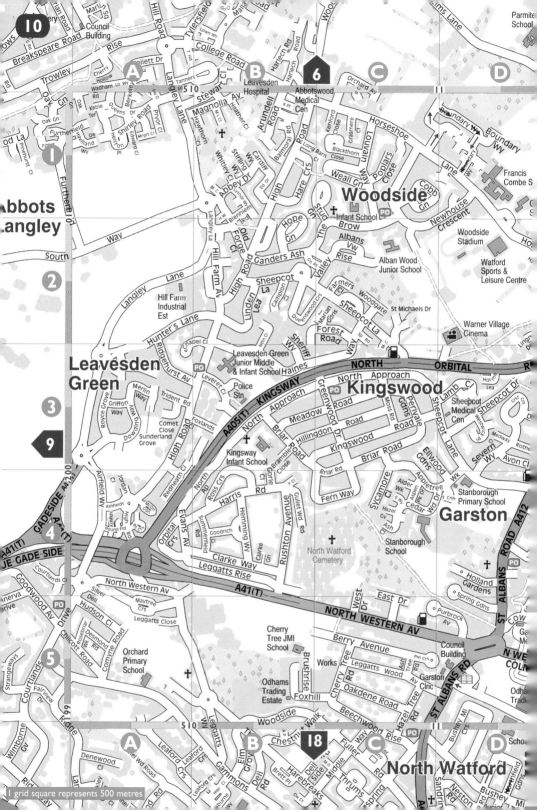

Wood

st Herts
matorium

Cemetery

E A405(T)

F

7

G

H

chaels
chool

Primary
School

Lych
Gate

PO

St
Albans
Road

Bucknalls Cl

Bucknalls   Lane

Tudor Mnr
Gdns

Coates

Bridger
Cl

Kytes   Dr

Coates   Way

Coates
Way Prim Sch

Lemon
Field Drive

Avalon

Cranefield Drive

Chichester Wy

Verdure
Close

Mutchetts Cl

Coates
Dell

I

Bricket
Wood
Common

School Lane

10

Little M
Farm

2

School Lane

Gaddesden Crs

Bovingdon
Crs

Codicote Drive

Felden Cl

Cuffley

Kimpton

Peregrine Cl

Bramfield

Kestrel Cl

Falcon   Way

Ravenscroft

3

12

200

Ver-Colne Valley Walk

4

Crab

ST ALBANS RD

N-ORBITAL-ROAD-ST-ALBANS-ROAD

Garston La

Garston La

Amwell

Garston
Station

The Gossamers

Ver-Colne Valley Walk

Univer
Hertfo

Woodhurst
Av

Telford

Third Av

Fourth Avenue

Whitwell
Rd

Phillipers

Tibbles Cl

Fairfolds

Garston
JMI
School

The Pelhams

Ninghoe

Lea
Bushes

Butterwick

Bowmans Gn

Meriden

5

ea Farm
unior
chool

Aldbury Cl

Phillipers

Bowmans
Gn

PO

The
Turnstones

Harvest
End

York

Carsmouth Way

Gadswell
Cl

Way

Kelshall

199

Meriden
Primary School

Capital
Business Cen

E A41(T)

The Wenta
Business Cen

N-WESTERN

Meriden Wy

Widford Wy

F Westlea Av

Eastlea Avenu

19

M1

River Colne

G

Otterspool

H

Walk

Douglas Av

12

A   B   C   D

514   15

Drop Lane

Bricket Wood Common

1

River Colne

Netherwyde Farm

Ver-Colne Valley Walk

School Lane

Little Munden Farm

Hill Farm

2

Oakridge Lane

3

Crab Lane

Blackbirds

11

La

Kemprow

Colne Valley Walk

4

Crab

Lane

Crab

Blackbirds Farm

Blackbirds Lane

Kemprow

University of Hertfordshire

B462

5

Fair Field Junior School

Kendal

Kemprow

High Cross

New

Batch

514   15

A   B   C   D

20 Grove

High

Edge Grove School

Red

1 grid square represents 500 metres

E   F   HARPER LANE B556   G   H

Hospital

Way

The Common

Radlett Lodge School

16

I

Houndswood

Wild Farm

10

Hambling

WD7

Brook Dr

Watling Knoll The Cl

Oakridge

Medow

Kitswell Wy

Works

Goodyers

Links

Av

The Heath

Beech

Avenue

The Warren

Park Av

Business Centre

Ldg End

Avenue

The Woods

Golf Course

2

Newlands

Avenue

Drive

Penne Cl

The Grove

Works

The

Regents Cl

Cary Wk

Aldenham Cv

Mornington

Hethy Rd

Lamoma Cl

The Sycamores

Porters Park Golf Club

Shenley Hill

3

Avenue

Park Rd

ROAD

Abbey View

Scotscraig

Highnds

The Cha Cl

Infant School

Station Rd

ROMAN ROAD

Radlett Station

Barn

High

Firs

Gills Hill

Rd

ALDENHAM RD

Beaumont

Scrambled

Rd

Radlett Pk Rd

Hillside Rd

Shenley

Shenley Hill

Canons Cl

Williams Av

Williams Wy

Faggots Cl

Williams Way

200

Shenley Rd

4

Gills Hollow

Gills

The Dell

Scrubbitts Park Road

Radlett & Bushey Reform Synagogue

PO

Surgery

The Crossways

Newberries Avenue

Craigwell Av

Newberries Av

RADLETT

Elm Walk

Woodfield Rd

Surgery

Letchmore Road

Council Building

Avenue

Slade Ct

Craig Mt.

Theobald Street

5

Christ Ch

Church Cl

Loom Pl

Cemetery

Theobald St

Aldenham

The Pathway

Loom Lane

The Rose Wk

COBDEN HILL

Radlett Infant School

Tabard RFC

Radlett Cricket Club

Martreys

Homefield Rd

Ridgeway

Homefield Rd

E   F   16   21   G   17   H

A5

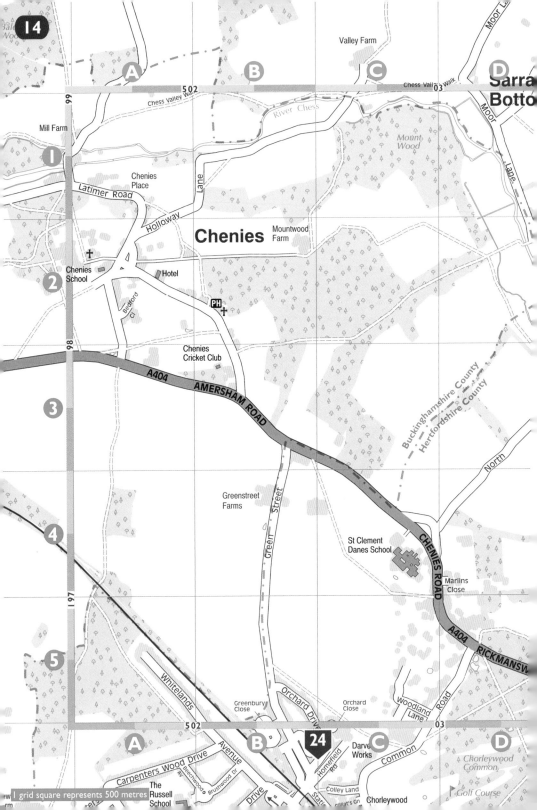

14

Dawes
Jowner
Alex
Rd
George Wy
Caroon Drive
Dimmocks Lane
Deadman's
PO
Sarrat School
Clutterbucks Lane
Surgery Lane

Newhall Farm

E
04
F
G
05
H
99

I

Church
Green End Business Centre

Goldingtons
PH
Micklefield Green
M25
2

Church End

Sarratt Mill House
New Road
98
Sarratt Road

3
Sarratt Road

16

Solesbridge Lane
4

Solesbridge Lane
Sarratt Lane
Cherry Walk
Beechengrove Wood
97

Chess Valley Walk

Ladywood Close
5

Solesbridge Close
The Readings
Chess Wy
Whisper Wood
Cherry Hl
Loudwater Hts
Bridle Lane
Lower Plantation
Wagon Way

Warwick Ct
Solesbridge La
Wyatt's Road
Tollgate Cl
Wyatt's Cl
Briery Fld
M25
River Chess
Trout Rise
Cherry Hl
Farm Way
Sarratt Lane
Lower Plantation

Loud

Church
E
A404
RICKMANSWORTH ROAD
High View
F
25
Junction 18
G
Troutstream
Kln
Overstr
Way
H
Loudwater Drive
Violet Rd
Lodge Dr
Timber Rdg
Rooks Hill
Armitage Close
Chess Chess Hill

Finch Green
Beechwood
Pk
Marriott Terrace
04
05

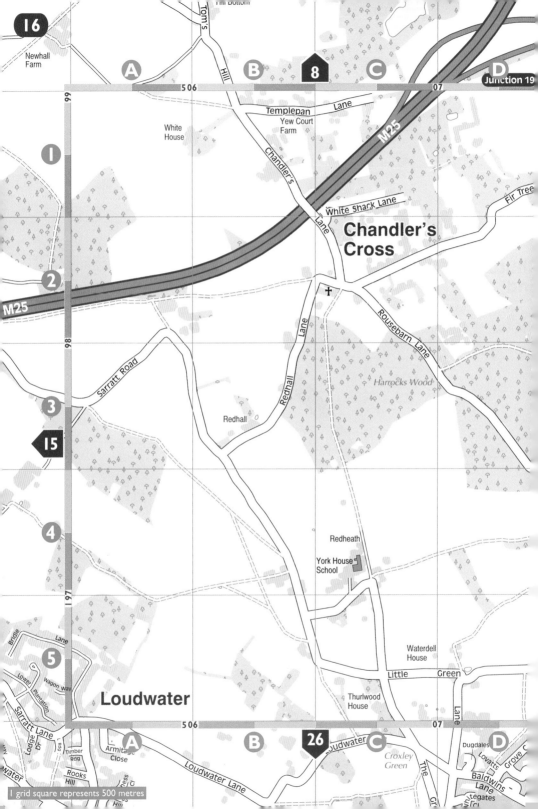

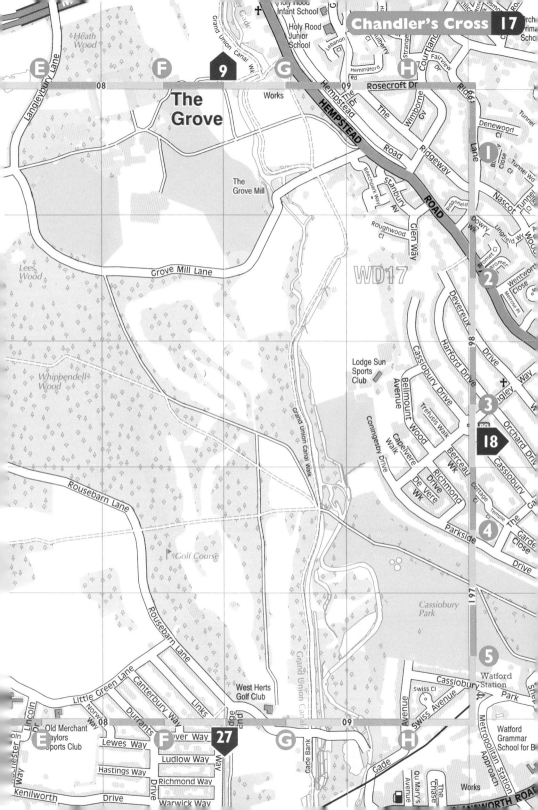

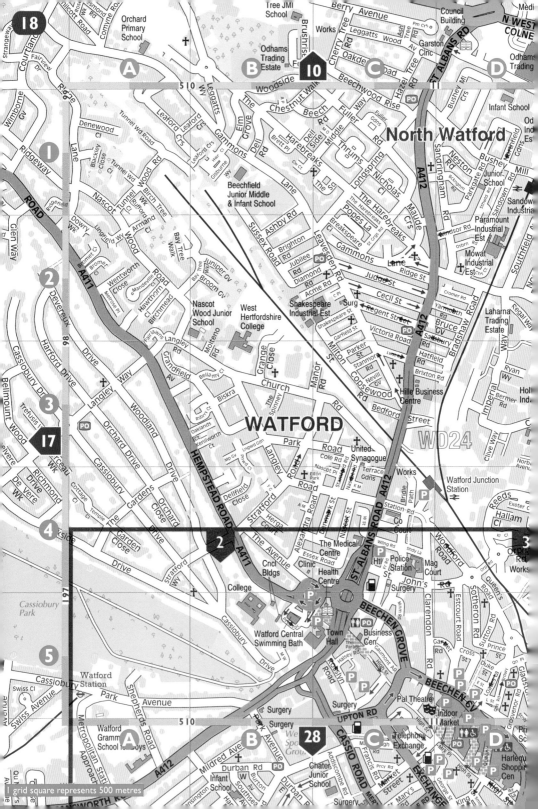

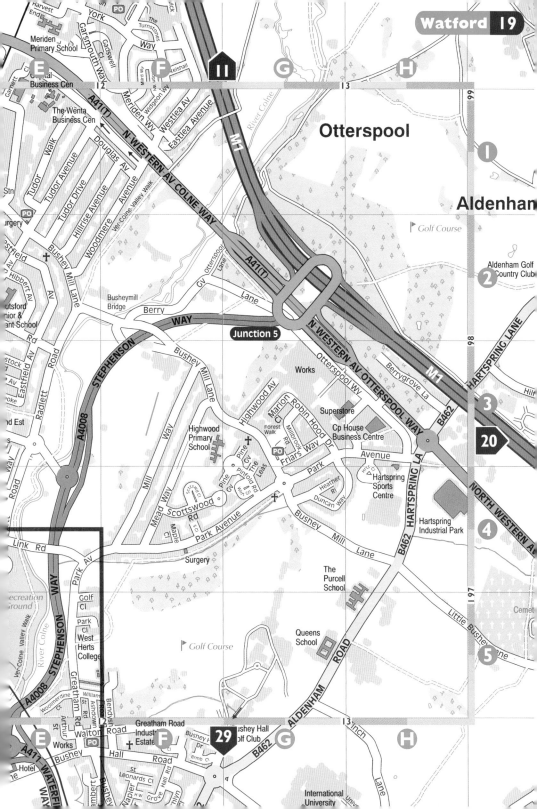

E

F

II

G

H

I

Otterspool

Aldenham

Golf Course

Harvest End

York

PO

The Turnstones

Kelshall

Meriden Primary School

Gadswell

Garsmouth Way

Widgeon Wy

Milrw Wy

Meriden Wy

Westlea Av

Eastlea Avenue

Way

River Colne

M1

Central Business Cen

Carnett

Cl

The Wenta Business Cen

A41(T)

N WESTERN AV COLNE WAY

Douglas Av

Tudor Walk

Tudor Avenue

Tudor Drive

Hilrise Avenue

Woodmere Avenue

Ver-Colne Valley Walk

Stn

PO

urgery

Estfield

Hibbert Av

utsford nior & nt School

Bushey Mill Lane

Eastfield Av

Radlett Road

Busheymill Bridge

Berry

Lane

WAY

Gv

Otterspool Lane

A41(T)

Lane

Gv

99

2

Aldenham Golf & Country Club

98

M1

Berrygrove La

N WESTERN AV OTTERSPOOL WAY

B462

Hartspring Lane

3

20

4

5

197

STEPHENSON

WAY

A4008

Mill Way

Bushey Mill Lane

Junction 5

Works

Otterspool Wy

Highwood Av

Marion Cl

Robin Hood Dr

Forest Walk

Pine

Gv

Pine

The Leas

PO

Pinfold Rd

Scottswood

Win Cl

Scottswood Rd

Mead Way

Maple Cl

Highwood Primary School

Pine Gv

Millbrook Rd

Friars Way

Superstore

Cp House Business Centre

Avenue

Park

Heather Rd

Duncan Way

Hrts Cl

Hartspring Sports Centre

Hartspring Industrial Park

Bushey Mill Lane

Little Bushey Lane

Cemet

Link Rd

WAY

A4008

STEPHENSON

Park Av

Park Avenue

Surgery

Golf Cl

Park Cl

West Herts College

River Colne

Ver-Colne Valley Walk

Golf Course

The Purcell School

Queens School

B462

ALDENHAM

ROAD

Recreation Ground

Greatham Rd

Woolmerdine Ct

William St

Arthur St

Ashdown

Bendysh Rd

Walton Road

Hall Road

PO

Works

St Leonards Cl

Grove Rd

HW

Rd

Napier St

A411 WATERFI

Hotel

Bushey

Greatham Road Industrial Estate

Bushey Hall Dr

Brmb

F

29

Bushey Hall Golf Club

G

B462

13 inch

H

Lane

Univ

International University

E

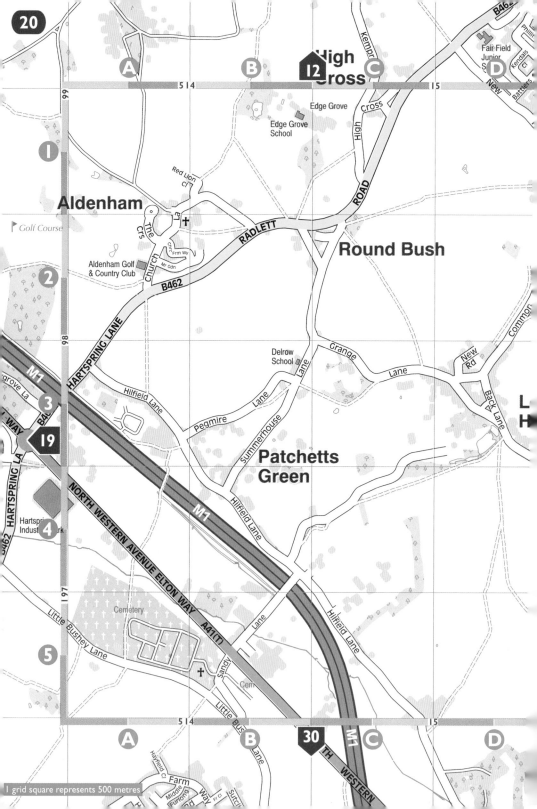

Elm
Walk

Cragg
Av

Cemetery

Church
Cl

E

The Pathway

Avenue

Aldenham

Len
Road

Loom Lane

F

13

COBDEN HILL

ett
School

G

The
Rose
Wk

17

H

Theobald Street

Loom Lane

Heyford
Rd

Homefield Rd

Homefield
Rd

Maytrees

The Ridgeway

The

Manor Ct

A5183

Tabard
RFC

Radlett
Cricket
Club

Tykes Water

I

Batlers
Green

Little Kendals
Farm

Hertsmere Jewish
Primary School

Radlett
Preparatory
School

2

86

Theobald Str

ore

A5183

3

22

Aldenham
School

m Road

A5183

Slades
Farm

North Medburn
Farm

4

Butterfly Lane

197

Elstree
Golf C

Elstree Aerodrome

Haberdashers' Aske's
Boys' School

5

E

16

F

Hogg Lane

31

G

17

Haberdashers' Aske's
Girls' School

H

Water

A5183

Dagger

Home

Green Street

BOREHAMWOOD

WD6

SHENLE

Hertsmere ish Primary School

Elstree Golf Club

Golf Course

Elstree Golf Club

N Medburn F

kes Water ke

Theobald Street

Theobald street

Theobald St

Parkside Prim School

The Campions

Lyndhurst Middle School

Merryfield School

Haberdashers RUFC

Council Building

Elstree Studios

Kinetic Business Centre

Boulevard 25 Retail Park

Elstree & Borehamwood Station

Harkness Industrial Est

Works

Works

Surgery

Surgery

Surgery

Stapleton Road

Walshford Way

Mirsk

Aycliffe Roa

Digswell

Greenside

Woolmer

Retford Cl

Berwick Road

Morpeth Avenue

Stretton Wy

Allerton Road

Belford Rd

Buckton Rd

Allerton Rd

Allerton Road

Torworth Rd

Leeming Road

Clifton Wy

Gateshead

Brook

Waterford Wy

Ranskill Rd

Norton

Grove Rd

Haggerston Road

Rosington Road

Wetherby Rd

Cromwell

Darlington Road

McKell Wy

Sinderby Cl

Aycliffe

Blyth

Gateshead Road

Catterick Wy

Croxdale Rd

Linton Avenue

Beech Drive

Merryfield Cl

Theobald St

Croxdale Road

Aberford Rd

Barton Wy

Chandos Road

Tallis Wy

Bairstow Cl

Stanley Gdns

Open Hall Rd

Gibbons Cl

Boyce Cl

Lombardy Wy

Stevenage Crescent

Frnt Wy

Beechfield

Anthony Road

Ashdown Dr

Kingsley AV

Maxwell Lodge

Red Road

Gables Av

Theobald St

Strattfield

Malden Rd

Essex Rd

Ling Cl

Haddon Wy

Barton Road

Glenhaven Av

Park Crs

Links Dr

Barham Avenue

Station Rd

Drayton Rd

Holt Cl

Blattner Close

Allum

B5378

1 grid square represents 500 metres

A5183

A 518 B C hurst 19 D

66 98 197

1
2
3
21
4
5

22
32

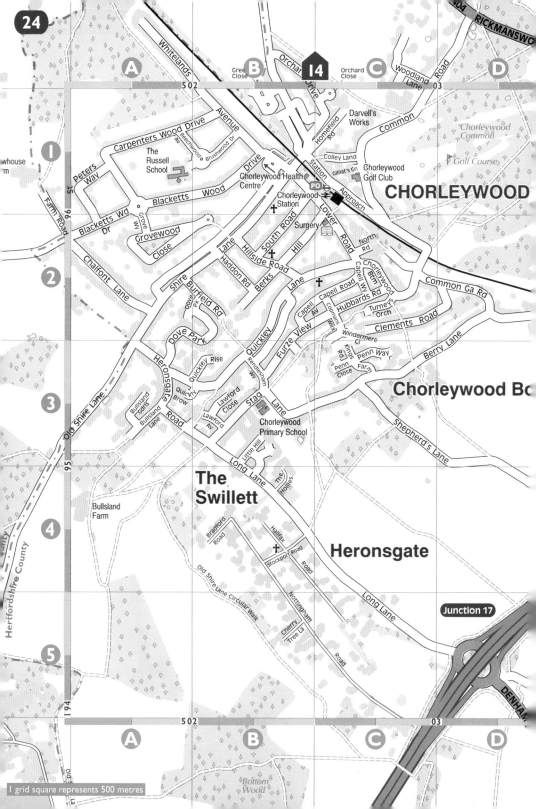

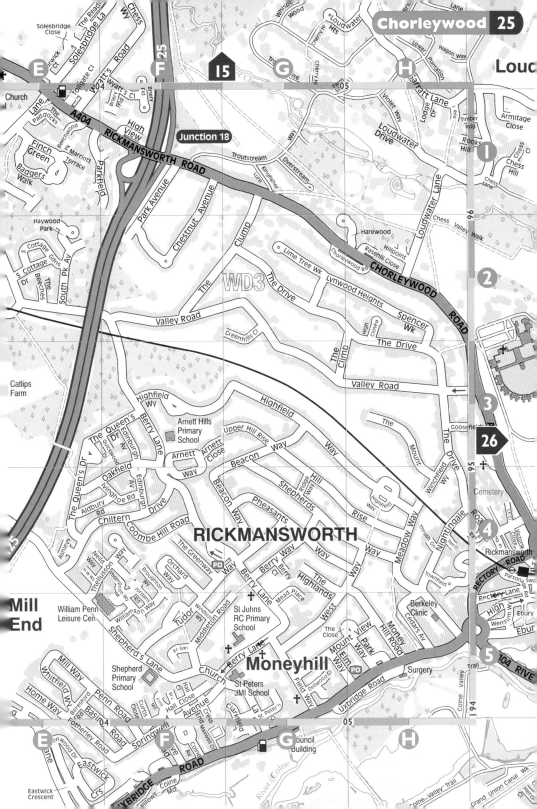

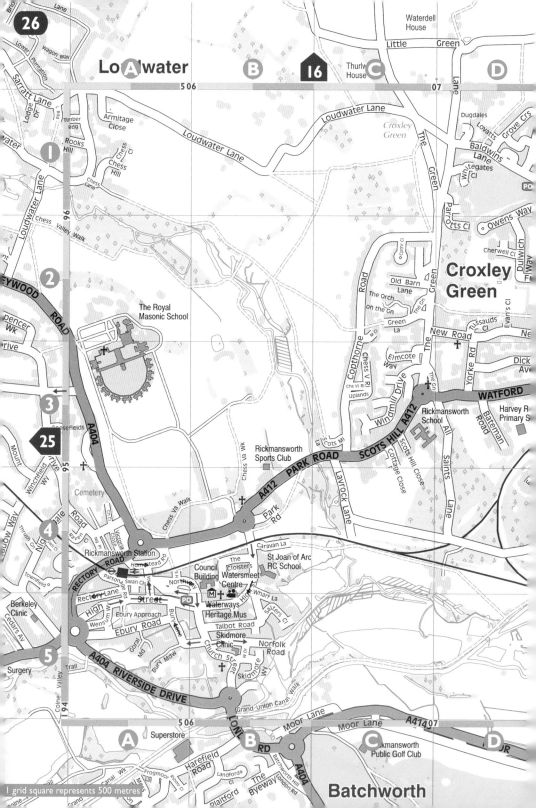

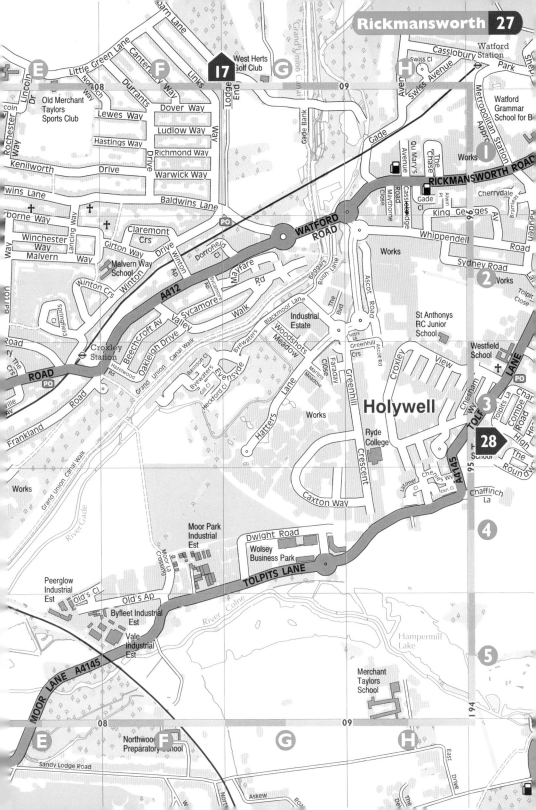

Watford
Station

Cassiobury
Park

Swiss Cl

E
Little Green Lane
Lincoln Dr
Rochester Way
Kenilworth Drive

F
Canterbury Way
Durrants
Norfolk Way
Lewes Way
Hastings Way
Dover Way
Ludlow Way
Richmond Way
Warwick Way

Links
Lodge End
Way

17

West Herts
Golf Club

G

Grand Union Canal

Gade Bank

Gade

H
Swiss Avenue
Avenue
Swiss Avenue

Metropolitan Station
Watford Approach

Watford
Grammar
School for B

Old Merchant
Taylors
Sports Club

twins Lane

rborne Way
Winchester Way
Malvern Way

Lancing Way
Girton Way
Claremont Crs
Malvern Way School
Winton Crs
Winton

Baldwins Lane

PO

Drive

Winton Ap

A412

Dorrofield Cl
Mayfare Rd
Sycamore Walk
Sycamore Valley

Beechcroft Av
Oakleigh Drive
Hazelwood Rd

Croxley
Station

ROAD
PO

Frankland Road

Grand Union Canal Walk

River Cade

Works

Peerglow
Industrial
Est

Old's Cl
Old's Ap

Byfleet Industrial
Est

Vale
Industrial
Est

MOOR LANE A4145

Grand Union

Canal Walk

Basildon Cl
Byewaters
Heckford Cl

Evensyde
Harters Lane

Woodshots
Meadow

Blackmoor Lane

Industrial
Estate

Beggars
Bush Lane

The Bvd

Martins Meadow
Faraday Close

Works

Moor La Crossing

Moor Park
Industrial
Est

Dwight Road

Wolsey
Business Park

TOLPITS LANE

River Colne

Northwood
Preparatory School

Sandy Lodge Road

Askew

WATFORD ROAD

RICKMANSWORTH ROAD

Qu Mary's Avenue
The Chase
Works

Cassiobridge Road
Maythorne

Gade

Alwin Pl
King George's Av

Cherrydale

Bramley

Hayden

Whippendell Road

Sydney Road

2
Works
Tolpit Close

I

Works

Ascot Road

Greenhill Crs
Ascot Rd

St Anthonys
RC Junior
School

Greenhill

Croxley View

Chesham Wy

Westfield
School

TOLPITS LANE

PO

Tolpits La

Combe Road
High

3

28

A4145

Chaffinch La

4

Latimer
Chenies Wy
Dkn Cl

Ryde
College

Crescent

Caxton Way

Holywell

Works

Hampermill
Lake

Merchant
Taylors
School

East Drive

The

Roundway

Char

5

E

F

G

H

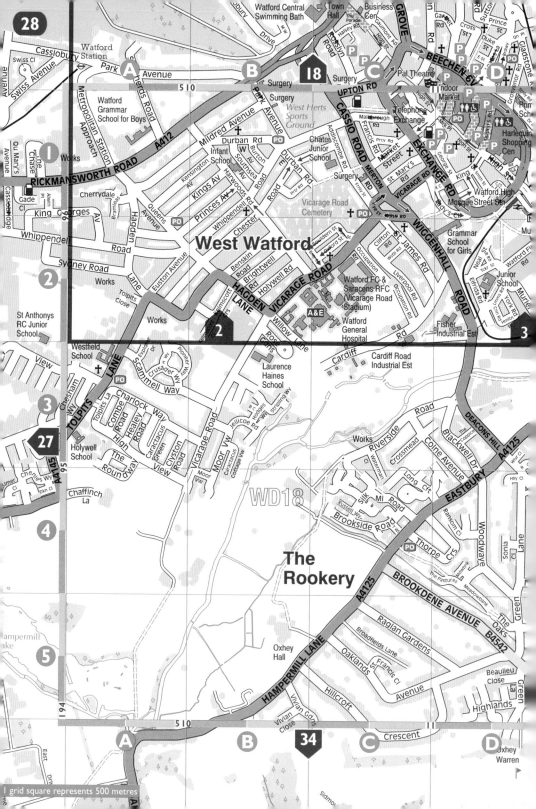

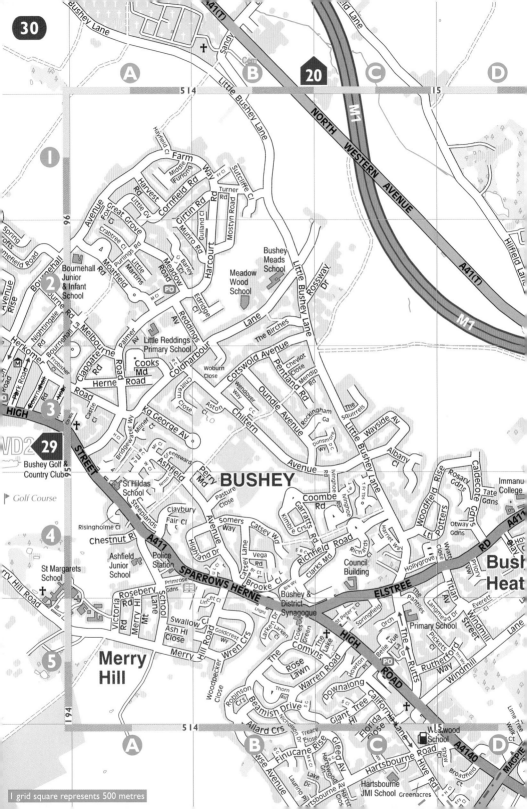

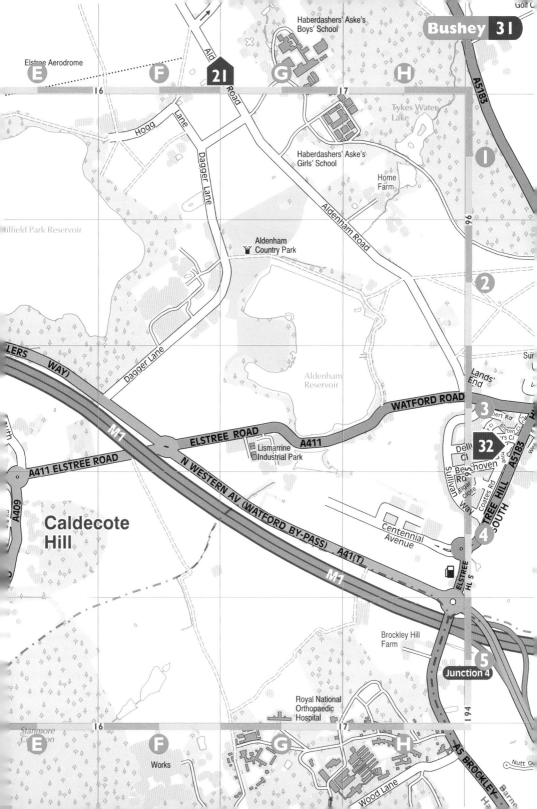

Golf C

Elstree Aerodrome

E 16 **F** 21 **G** 17 **H**

Haberdashers' Aske's Boys' School

A5183

Hogg Lane

Ald Road

Dagger Lane

Tykes Water Lake

I

Haberdashers' Aske's Girls' School

Home Farm

ilfield Park Reservoir

Aldenham Country Park

Aldenham Road

2

LERS WAY)

Dagger Lane

Aldenham Reservoir

Lands' End

WATFORD ROAD

3

M1

ELSTREE ROAD

A411

32

A5183

Deli Cl

Beethoven Rd

A411 ELSTREE ROAD

Lismarrine Industrial Park

N WESTERN AV (WATFORD BY-PASS) A41(T)

Sullivan Way

Elgar Close

Coates Rd

TREE HILL SOUTH

A409

Caldecote Hill

Centennial Avenue

4

M1

ELSTREE HL S

Brockley Hill Farm

5

Junction 4

A 194

Stanmore Co on

E 16 **F** **G** **H**

Works

Royal National Orthopaedic Hospital

Wood Lane

A5 BROCKLEY

Barne

Nutt C

Sur

BOREHAMWOOD

Elstree

Deacons Hill

Junction 4

1 grid square represents 500 metres

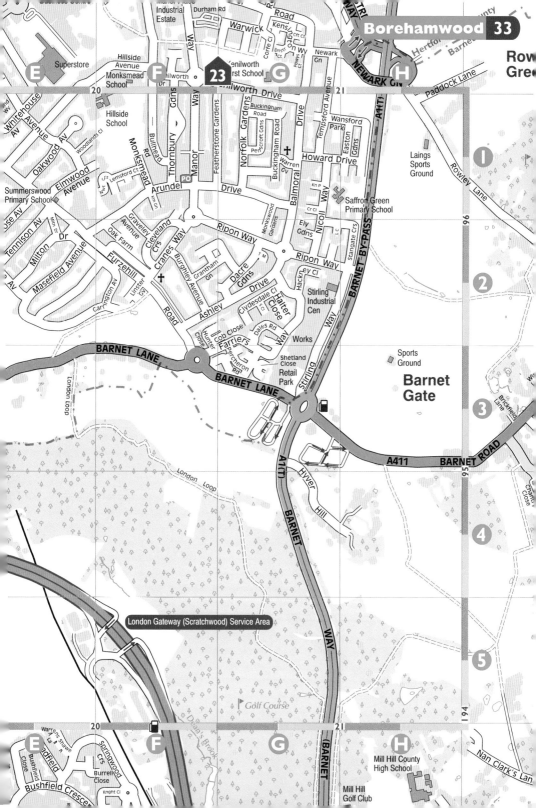

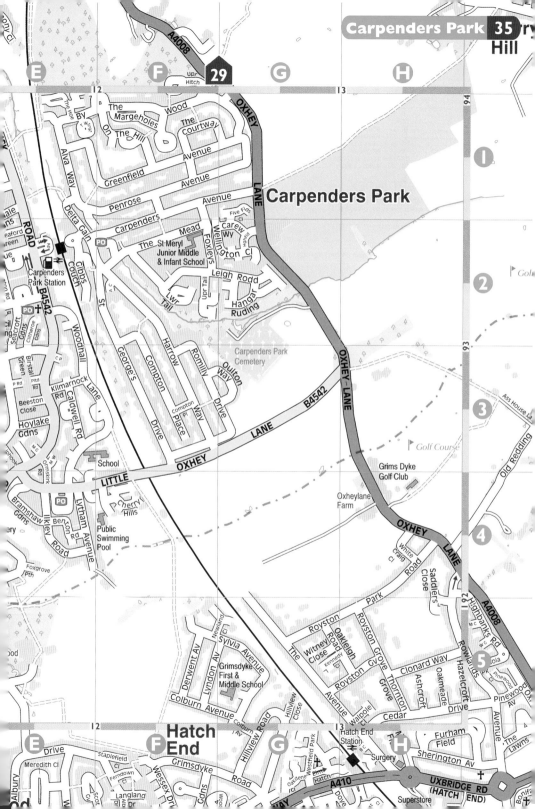

E   F   29   G   H

A4008

Upr. Hitch

12   13   94

Carpenders Park

I

Golf

The Hoe

The Margeholes

Wood

The Courtway

On The Hill

BV

Avenue

Greenfield

Alva Way

Delta Gain

Penrose

Avenue

Avenue

2

Carpenders

Mead

Five Flds. Cl.

PO

Carew Wy

Wellington Cl

OXHEY LANE

The St Meryl Junior Middle & Infant School

Foxleys

Gibbs Couch

Carpenders Park Station

Leigh Rodd

ROAD

Upr Tail

Hangar Ruding

Lwr Tail

B4542

PO

St

A C

Harrow

Romilly

Oulton Way

Carpenders Park Cemetery

George's

Compton

Way

Drive

Woodhall Lane

Compton Pl

3

OXHEY LANE B4542

Ass House La

Kilmarnock Rd

Caldwell Rd

Cilmeroe

Drive

Golf Course

Old Redding

Beeston Close

Hoylake Gdns

School

LITTLE

LANE

OXHEY

Grims Dyke Golf Club

93

4

Ilkley Avenue

PO

Lytham Avenue

Benton Rd

Cherry Hills

Public Swimming Pool

Oxheylane Farm

OXHEY LANE

White Craig Cl

Park

Saddlers Close

A4008

Highbanks Rd

Bramshaw Gdns

Foxgrove Pth

Road

5

Royston

Witney Close

Royston Road

Oakleigh

Kennedy

Royston Grove

Thornton Grove

Clonard Way

Ashcroft

Oakmeade

Hazelcroft

Rowlands

Pinewood AV

OX

Newland

Sylvia Avenue

Derwent Av

Lyndon Av

Grimsdyke First & Middle School

The

Avenue

Walpole

Cedar

Drive

Furham Field

Pinewood Avenue

The Lawns

Colburn Avenue

Colburn

Hillview Close

Hatch End Station

Sherington Av

12   13

E   F **Hatch End**   G   H

Drive

Staplefield

Meredith Cl

Ferndown Cl

Grimsdyke Road

Hillview Road

Westfield Park

Surgery

UXBRIDGE RD (HATCH END)

Hatch

A410

Superstore

Wessex Dr

Langland Dr

Doye

Abbots Langley	9 H1	Chorleywood Bottom	24 C3	Kingswood	10 C3	Radlett	1
Aldenham	19 H1	Church End	15 E2	Langleybury	9 E3	Rickmansworth	2
Barnet Gate	33 H3	Croxley Green	26 D2	Leavesden Green	9 H3	The Rookery	2
Batlers Green	21 E2	Deacons Hill	32 D3	Letchmore Heath	20 D3	Round Bush	2
Bedmond	5 H1	Eastbury	34 A3	Loudwater	16 A5	South Oxhey	3
Borehamwood	22 B5	Elstree	32 B3	Meriden	11 F5	The Swillett	2
Bricket Wood	7 F5	Garston	10 D4	Merry Hill	30 A5	Waterdale	
Bushey	30 B4	Green Street	22 D1	Micklefield Green	15 F2	Watford	
Bushey Heath	30 D4	The Grove	17 F1	Mill End	25 E5	Watford Heath	2
Caldecote Hill	31 E4	Heronsgate	24 C4	Moneyhill	25 C5	Well End	2
Carpenters Park	35 G1	High Cross	12 C5	North Watford	18 C1	West Watford	
Chandler's Cross	16 C2	Holywell	27 H3	Otterspool	19 G1	Woodside	1
Chenies	14 B2	Hunton Bridge	9 E2	Oxhey	29 E3		
Chorleywood	24 C1	Kings Langley	4 B2	Patchetts Green	20 B3		

USING THE STREET INDEX

Street names are listed alphabetically. Each street name is followed by its postal town or area locality, the Postcode District, the page number, and the reference to the square in which the name is found.

Standard index entries are shown as follows:

Abbey Dr *ABLGY* WD5 ....**10** B1

Street names and selected addresses not shown on the map due to scale restrictions are shown in the index with an asterisk:

Albany Ms *LCOL/BKTW* * AL2 ....**7** H1

GENERAL ABBREVIATIONS

ACC	ACCESS	E	EAST	LDG	LODGE	R	R
ALY	ALLEY	EMB	EMBANKMENT	LGT	LIGHT	RBT	ROUNDAB
AP	APPROACH	EMBY	EMBASSY	LK	LOCK	RD	R
AR	ARCADE	ESP	ESPLANADE	LKS	LAKES	RDG	R
ASS	ASSOCIATION	EST	ESTATE	LNDG	LANDING	REP	REPU
AV	AVENUE	EX	EXCHANGE	LTL	LITTLE	RES	RESER
BCH	BEACH	EXPY	EXPRESSWAY	LWR	LOWER	RFC	RUGBY FOOTBALL C
BLDS	BUILDINGS	EXT	EXTENSION	MAG	MAGISTRATE	RI	R
BND	BEND	F/O	FLYOVER	MAN	MANSIONS	RP	R
BNK	BANK	FC	FOOTBALL CLUB	MD	MEAD	RW	R
BR	BRIDGE	FK	FORK	MDW	MEADOWS	S	SC
BRK	BROOK	FLD	FIELD	MEM	MEMORIAL	SCH	SCH
BTM	BOTTOM	FLDS	FIELDS	MKT	MARKET	SE	SOUTH
BUS	BUSINESS	FLS	FALLS	MKTS	MARKETS	SER	SERVICE A
BVD	BOULEVARD	FLS	FLATS	ML	MALL	SH	SH
BY	BYPASS	FM	FARM	ML	MILL	SHOP	SHOP
CATH	CATHEDRAL	FT	FORT	MNR	MANOR	SKWY	SKY
CEM	CEMETERY	FWY	FREEWAY	MS	MEWS	SMT	SUN
CEN	CENTRE	FY	FERRY	MSN	MISSION	SOC	SOC
CFT	CROFT	GA	GATE	MT	MOUNT	SP	S
CH	CHURCH	GAL	GALLERY	MTN	MOUNTAIN	SPR	SP
CHA	CHASE	GDN	GARDEN	MTS	MOUNTAINS	SQ	SQ
CHYD	CHURCHYARD	GDNS	GARDENS	MUS	MUSEUM	ST	ST
CIR	CIRCLE	GLD	GLADE	MWY	MOTORWAY	STN	STA
CIRC	CIRCUS	GLN	GLEN	N	NORTH	STR	STR
CL	CLOSE	GN	GREEN	NE	NORTH EAST	STRD	STR
CLFS	CLIFFS	GRA	GROUND	NW	NORTH WEST	SW	SOUTH
CMP	CAMP	GRG	GRANGE	O/P	OVERPASS	TDG	TRA
CNR	CORNER	GT	GARAGE	OFF	OFFICE	TER	TER
CO	COUNTY	GTWY	GREAT	ORCH	ORCHARD	THWY	THROUGH
COLL	COLLEGE	GV	GATEWAY	OV	OVAL	TNL	TUI
COM	COMMON	HGR	GROVE	PAL	PALACE	TOLL	TOL
COMM	COMMISSION	HL	HIGHER	PAS	PASSAGE	TPK	TURN
CON	CONVENT	HLS	HILL	PAV	PAVILION	TR	T
COT	COTTAGE	HO	HILLS	PDE	PARADE	TRL	
COTS	COTTAGES	HOL	HOUSE	PH	PUBLIC HOUSE	TWR	T
CP	CAPE	HOSP	HOLLOW	PK	PARK	U/P	UNDER
CPS	COPSE	HRB	HOSPITAL	PKWY	PARKWAY	UNI	UNIVE
CR	CREEK	HTH	HARBOUR	PL	PLACE	UPR	U
CREM	CREMATORIUM	HTS	HEATH	PLN	PLAIN	V	
CRS	CRESCENT	HVN	HEIGHTS	PLNS	PLAINS	VA	V
CSWY	CAUSEWAY	HWY	HAVEN	PLZ	PLAZA	VIAD	VIA
CT	COURT	IMP	HIGHWAY	POL	POLICE STATION	VIL	
CTRL	CENTRAL	IN	IMPERIAL	PR	PRINCE	VIS	
CTS	COURTS	IND EST	INLET	PREC	PRECINCT	VLG	VII
CTYD	COURTYARD	INF	INDUSTRIAL ESTATE	PREP	PREPARATORY	VLS	V
CUTT	CUTTINGS	INFO	INFIRMARY	PRIM	PRIMARY	VW	V
CV	COVE	INT	INFORMATION	PROM	PROMENADE	W	
CYN	CANYON	IS	INTERCHANGE	PRS	PRINCESS	WD	V
DEPT	DEPARTMENT	JCT	ISLAND	PRT	PORT	WHF	W
DL	DALE	JTY	JUNCTION	PT	POINT	WK	V
DM	DAM	KG	JETTY	PTH	PATH	WKS	V
DR	DRIVE	KNL	KING	PZ	PIAZZA	WLS	V
DRO	DROVE	L	KNOLL	QD	QUADRANT	WY	V
DRY	DRIVEWAY	LA	LAKE	QU	QUEEN	YD	
DWGS	DWELLINGS		LANE	QY	QUAY	YHA	YOUTH H

POSTCODE TOWNS AND AREA ABBREVIATIONS

ABLGY	Abbots Langley	GSTN	Garston	LCOL/BKTW	London Colney/	RAD	
BAR	Barnet	HHS/BOV	Hemel Hempstead south/		Bricket Wood	RKW/CH/CXG	Rickmans
BORE	Borehamwood		Bovingdon	MLHL	Mill Hill		Chorleywood/Croxley
BUSH	Bushey	KGLGY	Kings Langley	NTHWD	Northwood	WAT	V
CSHM	Chesham	KTN/HRWW/WS	Kenton/Harrow Weald/	OXHEY	Oxhey	WATN	Watfor
CSTG	Chalfont St Giles		Wealdstone	PIN	Pinner	WATW	Watfor

A

ey Dr ABLGY WD5 ....10 B1
ey Vw RAD WD7 ....13 H4
ts Pl BORE WD6..........................23 E2
ts Ri KGLGY WD4 ....4 C1
ts Rd ABLGY WD5 ....5 F5
ts Vw KGLGY WD4 ....4 C3
ford Rd BORE WD6........................22 D4
e Rd WATN WD24 ....18 B2
n Pl WATN WD24 ....18 B1
scombe Rd WATW WD18 ....2 E4
ara Rd NTHWD HA6 ....34 A4
an Rd ABLGY WD5 ....5 H5
dale Rd OXHEY WD19..............35 D2
n Crs BORE WD6.........................23 E3
ns Vw GSTN WD25 ....10 C2
ny Cl BORE WD6..........................30 C5
ny Ms LCOL/BKTW * AL2 ....7 H1
rt Rd WAT WD17 ....3 F2
rt Rd South WATW WD18 ....2 E2
ury Cl GSTN WD25 ....11 E5
ury Rd RKW/CH/CXG WD3 ....25 E4
nham Av RAD WD7 ....21 F1
nham Ga RAD WD7 ....13 C3
nham Rd GSTN WD25 ....21 E4
HEY WD19 ....29 E3
O WD7 ....13 F4
r Wk GSTN WD25 ....10 C4
ndra Ms WAT WD17 ....18 A4
ndra Rd BORE WD6 ....4 D5
LGY WD4 ....4 D5
T WD17 ....1 D1
ton Cl BORE WD6........................22 C2
ton Rd BORE WD6 ....22 B2
nts Crs GSTN WD25.................11 E2
ints La RKW/CH/CXG WD3 ....26 D3
n La BORE WD6............................32 B2
nd Wy BORE WD6.......................23 F3
t Wy NTHWD HA6 ....34 A4
Wy OXHEY WD19 ....35 E1
i Pl WATW WD18 ....27 H1
n Cl BORE WD6............................32 C3

sham Rd
N/CH/CXG WD3 ....14 A3
l Cl GSTN WD25.........................11 F4
esey Rd OXHEY WD19 ....34 D4
ath Gn OXHEY WD19 ....34 B2
r Cl KGLGY WD4 ....4 C3
Cl BUSH WD23 ....31 E4
e Ct WATW * WD18 ....2 A5
Rd WAT WD17 ....18 B2
age Cl RKW/CH/CXG WD3 ....26 A1
t Cl RKW/CH/CXG WD3 ....25 F3
t Wy RKW/CH/CXG WD3 ....25 F3
Gn OXHEY WD19 ....35 E3
more Ct BUSH * WD23 ....29 F1
r St BUSH WD23 ....3 K4

oke Dell
N/CH/CXG * WD3 ....24 D1
tree Wk GSTN WD25 ....10 C4
rius Wy NTHWD HA6 ....34 B4
ath Gn OXHEY WD19 ....34 B2
ony Cl OXHEY WD19 ....29 E5
ony Rd BORE WD6.....................22 B4
nette Ct ABLGY * WD5 ....6 A3
o NTHWD HA6 ....34 B4
tree Dell
N/CH/CXG * WD3 ....25 E1
tree Wk GSTN WD25 ....10 C4
rius Wy NTHWD HA6 ....34 B4
ath Gn OXHEY WD19 ....34 B2
r Cl KGLGY WD4 ....4 C3
Cl BUSH WD23 ....31 E4
e Ct WATW * WD18 ....2 A5
t Rd WAT WD17 ....18 A2
age Cl RKW/CH/CXG WD3 ....26 A1
i Cl RKW/CH/CXG WD3 ....25 F3
t Wy RKW/CH/CXG WD3 ....25 F3
Gn OXHEY WD19 ....35 E3
more Ct BUSH * WD23 ....29 F1
r St BUSH WD23 ....3 K4

oke Dell
N/CH/CXG * WD3 ....24 D1
el Dr BORE WD6...........................33 F1
ell Rd ABLGY WD5 ....10 B1
Cl BORE WD6................................32 D2
Ct RKW/CH/CXG WD3 ....27 E3
Rd WATW WD18..........................27 H2
rnham Cl OXHEY * WD19 ....34 B2
rnham Dr OXHEY WD19...........34 B2
Rd WATN WD24...........................18 B2
ABLGY WD5 ....9 G1
WD25 ....10 C4
opse LCOL/BKTW AL2.............7 C5
ft PIN HA5......................................35 H5
wn Dr BORE WD6.......................33 F1
wn Rd BUSH WD23.....................3 K3
ld Av BUSH WD23 ....30 A3
ds GSTN WD25 ....10 A4
rd Ln GSTN WD25 ....10 A4
rd Ln OXHEY WD19 ....35 E4
Cl BUSH WD23 ....30 A5
Dr BORE WD6..............................33 F2
i Cl RKW/CH/CXG WD3 ....25 F4
Cl BUSH WD23 ....29 F1
ge Dr LCOL/BKTW AL2 ....7 F4
BUSH WD23 ....34 D4
ee Rd WATN WD24 ....10 C5
Park Dr GSTN WD25...................10 C4
Cl BUSH WD23 ....30 B3

WATN WD24 ....3 H1
Athlone Cl RAD * WD7 ....13 C5
Atria Rd NTHWD HA6..................34 B4
Attenborough Cl OXHEY WD19 ....35 F2
Audley Cl BORE WD6 ....22 D5
Austin Vls GSTN * WD25 ....6 C5
Avalon Cl GSTN WD25 ....11 F1
Avenue Ap KGLGY WD4 ....4 A4
Avenue Ri BUSH WD23 ....29 H2
Avenue Ter OXHEY WD19..........29 F3
The Avenue BUSH WD23 ....29 G1
   PIN HA5 ....35 C5
   RAD WD7 ....13 F4
   WAT WD17 ....2 D1
Avior Dr NTHWD HA6..................34 A3
Avon Cl GSTN WD25 ....10 D3
Awberry Ct WATW * WD18 ....27 C3
Aycliffe Rd BORE WD6 ....22 C3
Aynho St WATW WD18................2 E6

B

Back La GSTN WD25 ....20 D3
Badgers Cl BORE * WD6 ....22 D4
Badgers Wk RKW/CH/CXG WD3...25 E1
Badminton Cl BORE WD6 ....22 D4
Baird Cl BUSH WD23 ....30 A3
Bairstow Cl BORE WD6...............22 B3
Balcon Wy BORE WD6.................23 F3
Baldock Wy BORE WD6...............22 C3
Baldwins La RKW/CH/CXG WD3...26 D1
Ballater Cl OXHEY WD19 ....34 C3
Balmoral Dr BORE WD6 ....33 C1
Balmoral Rd GSTN WD25 ....10 B1
   WATN WD24 ....18 D2
Banbury St WATW WD18 ....2 D1
Bankside Down
   RKW/CH/CXG * WD3 ....26 A3
Banks Rd BORE WD6...................23 F4
Barclay Cl WATW WD18 ....28 B3
Barham Av BORE WD6 ....22 C5
Barley Cl BUSH WD23 ....30 A2
Barn Cl RAD WD7 ....13 F4
Barnes Ri KGLGY WD4 ....4 C1
Barnet By-Pass BORE WD6 ....33 H2
Barnet La BORE WD6...................32 C5
   BORE WD6 ....33 E1
Barnet Rd MLHL NW7 ....33 H3
Barnet Wy (Barnet By-Pass)
   MLHL NW7 ....33 G4
Barnhurst Pth OXHEY WD19.....34 D4
Barn Lea RKW/CH/CXG WD3.....25 F5
Barnsdale Cl BORE WD6 ....22 C3
Barnsway KGLGY WD4 ....4 C4
The Bartons BORE * WD6...........32 A3
Barton Wy BORE WD6..................22 D4
   RKW/CH/CXG WD3 ....27 E2
Basildon Cl WATW WD18 ....27 F3
Basing Rd RKW/CH/CXG WD3 ...25 E1
Bateman Rd RKW/CH/CXG WD3...26 D3
Battlers Green Dr RAD WD7 ......20 D1
Bayhurst Dr NTHWD HA6 ....34 A5
Bay Tree Wk WAT WD17 ....18 A2
Beacon Wy RKW/CH/CXG WD3...25 C4
Beagle Cl RAD WD7 ....21 E1
Beamish Dr BUSH WD23 ....30 B5
Beasant House WATN WD24.......3 J1
Beauchamp Gdns
   RKW/CH/CXG WD3 ....25 E1
Beaulieu Cl WATW WD10 ....28 C5
Beaumont Ga RAD WD7 ....13 F4
Bedford Cl RKW/CH/CXG WD3 ...14 A2
Bedford St WATN WD24 ....18 C3
Bedmond Rd ABLGY WD5............6 A3
Beech Av RAD WD7 ....13 F2
Beechcroft Av RKW/CH/CXG WD3 27 F5
Beechcroft Rd BUSH WD23........29 F2
Beech Dr BORE WD6 ....22 C4
Beechen Gv WAT WD17 ....2 E2
The Beeches RKW/CH/CXG WD3...25 E2
   WATW * WD18............................2 D4
Beechfield KGLGY WD4 ....4 C4
Beechfield Cl BORE WD6 ....22 B4
Beechpark Wy WAT WD17 ....17 H1
Beech Rd WATN WD24.................18 B1
Beechwood Av
   RKW/CH/CXG WD3 ....24 A1
Beechwood Pk
   RKW/CH/CXG WD3 ....25 E1
Beechwood Ri WATN WD24 ....10 C5
Beehive Cl BORE WD6.................32 A3
Beeston Cl OXHEY WD19............35 E5
Beethoven Rd BORE WD6...........31 H4
Beggars Bush La WATW WD18...27 G2
Beken Ct GSTN * WD25 ....10 D4
Belfairs OXHEY WD19 ....35 E4

Belford Rd BORE WD6.................22 C2
Belgrave Av WATW WD18 ....2 B7
Belham Rd KGLGY WD4 ....4 C2
Bellamy Cl WAT WD17 ....18 B3
Bell Cl ABLGY WD5 ....6 A1
Belle Vue La BUSH WD23 ....30 C5
Bell La ABLGY WD5 ....6 B1
Bellmount Wood Av WAT WD17 ...17 H3
Belmont Rd BUSH WD23.............29 F1
Belmor BORE WD6........................32 D2
Belvedere Gdns LCOL/BKTW AL2 ..7 C1
Bembridge Pl GSTN * WD25 ......10 B2
Bendysh Rd BUSH WD23 ....19 F5
Benskin Rd WATW WD18.............2 C6
Benton Rd OXHEY WD19 ....35 E4
Berceau Wk WAT WD17...............17 H3
Beresford Rd
   RKW/CH/CXG WD3 ....25 E5
Berkeley Cl ABLGY WD5 ....10 A1
   BORE WD6 ....32 D2
Berkeley Ct
   RKW/CH/CXG * WD3 ....27 G2
Berks Hl RKW/CH/CXG WD3 .....24 B2
Bermer Rd WATN WD24 ....18 D3
Berry Av WATN WD24..................10 C5
Berry Cl RKW/CH/CXG WD3 ......25 C4
Berry Grove La BUSH WD23 ......19 F2
Berrygrove La GSTN WD25 ....19 H3
Berry La RKW/CH/CXG WD3 .....24 C3
   RKW/CH/CXG WD3 ....25 C5
Berry Wy RKW/CH/CXG WD3 ...25 C4
Berwick Rd BORE WD6 ....22 C2
Biddenham Turn GSTN WD25 ...10 D4
Birch Copse LCOL/BKTW AL2 ....7 F4
The Birches BUSH WD23 ....30 B2
Birchmead WAT WD17 ....18 A2
Birch Tree Wk WAT WD17...........18 A1
Birch Wk BORE * WD6.................22 D3
Birkdale Gdns OXHEY WD19......35 E3
Birstal Gn OXHEY WD19..............35 E5
Bishops Av BORE WD6.................32 C2
Biskra WAT WD17.........................18 B3
Blackbirds La GSTN WD25..........12 B3
Black Boy Wd LCOL/BKTW AL2...7 H4
Blacketts Wood Dr
   RKW/CH/CXG WD3 ....24 A1
Blackford Rd OXHEY WD19 ....35 E4
Blackley Cl WAT WD17 ....18 A1
Blackmoor La WATW WD18 ....27 C2
Blackthorn Cl GSTN WD25 ....10 C1
Blackwell Dr OXHEY WD19.........28 D3
Blackwell Rd KGLGY WD4 ....4 D3
Blairhead Dr OXHEY WD19.........34 C2
Blattner Cl BORE WD6.................32 B1
Blenheim Cl OXHEY WD19..........28 D4
Blenheim Rd GSTN WD25 ....10 B2
Bluebell Dr ABLGY WD5................6 A1
Bluebird Wy LCOL/BKTW AL2 ....7 C4
Blyth Cl BORE WD6 ....22 C3
Bognor Gdns OXHEY * WD19 .....34 D4
Boulevard WATW * WD18 ....27 G2
The Boulevard WATW WD18.......27 C2
Boundary Wy GSTN WD25 ....10 C1
Bournehall Cl BUSH * WD23 ......29 H3
Bournehall Av BUSH WD23 ....29 H3
Bournehall La BUSH WD23 ....29 H3
Bournehall Rd BUSH WD23 ....29 H3
Bovingdon Crs GSTN WD25 ....11 E3
Bowmans Gn GSTN WD25 ....11 F5
Bowring Gn OXHEY WD19..........34 D4
Royce Cl BORE WD6.....................22 B3
Brackendene LCOL/BKTW AL2 .../ G4
Bradbury Cl BORE WD6...............23 E3
Bradford Rd
   RKW/CH/CXG WD3 ....24 B4
Bradshaw Rd WATN WD24 ....18 D3
Bramble Cl GSTN WD25 ....10 B3
Brambling Cl BUSH WD23 ....29 F1
Bramfield GSTN WD25.................11 F3
Bramleas WATW WD18 ....2 A6
Bramley Cl WATW WD18 ....2 A6
Bramley Gdns OXHEY WD19......34 D5
Brampton Cl OXHEY WD19.........34 B2
Brampton Ter BORE WD6 ....22 D2
Bramshaw Gdns OXHEY WD19 ..35 E4
Bray Cl BORE WD6 ....23 F3
Breakspear Ct ABLGY WD5 ....6 A4
Breakspeare Cl WATN WD24 ......18 C2
Breakspeare Rd ABLGY WD5 ....5 H5
Brendon Ct RAD * WD7 ....13 G3
Brett Pl WATN WD24 ....18 B1
Briar Rd GSTN WD25 ....10 B3
Brick Kiln Cl BUSH WD23 ....29 F3
Bridge Ct RAD * WD7 ....13 G4
Bridge Pl WAT WD17 ....3 J7
Bridger Cl GSTN WD25 ....11 E2
Bridge Rd KGLGY WD4 ....9 F2

Bridgewater Wy BUSH WD23 .....30 A3
Bridle La RKW/CH/CXG WD3......15 H5
Bridle Pth WAT WD17 ....18 C4
Bridlington Rd OXHEY WD19 .....35 E2
Briery Fld RKW/CH/CXG WD3....15 F5
Brighton Rd WATN WD24 ....18 B2
Brightview Cl LCOL/BKTW AL2....7 F3
Brightwell Rd WATW WD18...........2 C7
Britten Cl BORE WD6...................32 A3
Brixton Rd WATN WD24...............18 C3
Broad Acre LCOL/BKTW AL2 ......7 F4
Broadfields La OXHEY WD19......28 C5
The Broadway WAT WD17..............3 H3
Brocklesbury Cl WATN WD24 ......3 H2
Brodewater Rd BORE WD6 ....23 E4
Bromborough Gn OXHEY WD19 ..34 D4
Bromet Cl WAT WD17..................18 A2
Brook Ct RAD * WD7 ....13 F4
Brookdene Av OXHEY WD19 ......28 C4
Brook Dr RAD * WD7 ....13 E2
Brooke Cl BUSH WD23.................30 B4
Brooke Wy BUSH WD23..............30 B4
Brookmill Cl OXHEY * WD19 ......28 C4
Brook Rd BORE WD6 ....22 D3
Brookside WATN * WD24 ....11 E5
Brookside Rd OXHEY WD19 ....28 C4
Broomfield Rd ABLGY WD5 ....9 G1
Broom Gv WAT WD17 ....18 B2
Broughinge Rd BORE WD6..........23 E4
Broughton Wy
   RKW/CH/CXG WD3 ....25 F4
Brownlow Rd BORE WD6.............32 D1
The Brow GSTN WD25 ....10 C3
Bruce Gv WATN WD24.................18 C2
Brushrise WATN WD24.................10 B5
Brushwood Dr
   RKW/CH/CXG WD3 ....24 B1
Buchanan Ct BORE * WD6...........23 F4
Buckettsland La BORE WD6........23 G2
Buckingham Rd BORE WD6.........33 C1
   WATN WD24 ....18 D1
Bucklands OXHEY * WD19 ....35 E2
Bucknalls Cl GSTN WD25 ....11 F1
Bucknalls Dr LCOL/BKTW AL2....7 G5
Bucknalls La GSTN WD25 ....11 F1
Bucks Av OXHEY WD19 ....29 F4
Bucks Hl KGLGY WD4....................8 A4
Buckton Rd BORE WD6................22 C2
Bullhead Rd BORE WD6...............23 F4
Bullsland Gdns
   RKW/CH/CXG WD3 ....24 A3
Bullsland La RKW/CH/CXG WD3...24 A3
Burchell Ct BUSH WD23 ....30 B4
Burfield Rd RKW/CH/CXG WD3 ..24 A2
Burghley Av BORE WD6 ....33 F2
Burleigh Ct BUSH * WD23 ....29 F1
Burn Cl GSTN * WD25 ....30 C1
Burnley Cl OXHEY WD19..............34 D4
Burton Av WATW WD18 ....2 D4
Bury La RKW/CH/CXG WD3........26 A5
Bury Mdw RKW/CH/CXG WD3 ...26 A5
Bushey Grove Rd BUSH WD23.....3 K4
Bushey Hall Dr BUSH WD23 ....29 F1
Bushey Hall Pk BUSH * WD23 ....29 F1
Bushey Hall Rd BUSH WD23.........3 K4
Busheymill Br BUSH WD23..........19 F2
Bushey Mill Crs WATN WD24......18 D1
Bushey Mill La BUSH WD23 ....19 C4
   WATN WD24 ....18 D1
Butterfly La BORE WD6................21 G5
Buttermere Pl GSTN * WD25 .....10 B2
Butterwick GSTN WD25 ....11 F5
Buxton Pth OXHEY * WD19 ....34 D5
Byewaters WATW WD18 ....27 F3
Byron Av BORE WD6 ....32 D2
   WATN WD24 ....19 E3
By the Wood OXHEY WD19 ....35 E1

C

Caishowe Rd BORE WD6.............23 E3
Caldecote Gdns BUSH WD23 .....30 D3
Caldecote La BUSH WD23 ....31 E4
Caldwell Rd OXHEY WD19...........35 E4
California La BORE WD6 ....33 C5
The Callanders BUSH * WD23....30 D5
Callowland Pl WATN WD24 ....18 C2
Cambridge Rd WATW WD18..........3 C5
Campion Cl GSTN WD25 ....10 B2
The Campions BORE WD6 ....22 C2
Cannon Rd WATW WD18................3 H7
Canons Cl RAD WD7.....................13 G4
Canopus Wy NTHWD HA6 ....34 A3
Canterbury Cl NTHWD HA6 ....34 A5
Canterbury Rd BORE WD6 ....22 D4
   WAT * WD17 ....18 C4

Canterbury Wy
RKW/CH/CXG WD3 ....17 F5
Capella Rd *NTHWD* HA6 ....34 A4
Capell Av *RKW/CH/CXG* WD3 .....24 B2
Capell Rd *RKW/CH/CXG* WD3 .....24 C2
Capell Wy *RKW/CH/CXG* WD3.....24 C2
Capel Rd *OXHEY* WD19 ....29 E3
Capelvere Wk *WAT* WD17 ....17 H3
Caractacus Cottage Vw
WATW WD18 ....28 B4
Caractacus Gn *WATW* WD18 ....28 A3
Caravan La *RKW/CH/CXG* WD3 ...26 B4
Cardiff Rd *WATW* WD18 ....28 C3
Cardiff Wy *ABLGY* WD5 ....10 B1
Cardinal Av *BORE* WD6 ....23 E5
Carew Wy *OXHEY* WD19 ....35 G2
Carisbrooke Av *WATN* WD24 ....19 E3
Carlton Cl *BORE* WD6 ....33 G1
Caroline Pl *OXHEY* WD19 ....29 F3
Carpenders Av *OXHEY* WD19 ......35 F2
Carpenters Wood Dr
RKW/CH/CXG WD3.....................24 A1
Carrington Av *BORE* WD6 ....33 E2
Cart Pth *GSTN* WD25 ....10 D2
Cary Wk *RAD* WD7 ....13 G3
Cassiobridge Rd *WATW* WD18 ....27 H1
Cassiobridge Ter
RKW/CH/CXG * WD3 ....27 G2
Cassiobury Dr *WAT* WD17 ....17 H3
Cassiobury Park Av
WATW WD18 ....17 H5
Cassio Rd *WATW* WD18 ....2 E4
Cassio Whf *WATW* * WD18 ....27 G2
Castle Cl *BUSH* WD23 ....30 A3
Catsey La *BUSH* WD23 ....30 B4
Catsey Wd *BUSH* WD23 ....30 B4
Catterick Wy *BORE* WD6...............22 C3
Cavendish Ct
RKW/CH/CXG * WD3 ....27 G2
Cavendish Crs *BORE* WD6............32 D1
Caxton Wy *WATW* WD18................27 G4
Cecil St *WATN* WD24.....................18 C2
Cedar Dr *PIN* HA5.........................35 H5
Cedar Rd *OXHEY* WD19 ....28 D3
Cedars Av *RKW/CH/CXG* WD3 .....25 H5
Cedars Cl *BORE* WD6 ....32 D1
Cedar Wood Dr *GSTN* WD25 ....10 C4
Centennial Av *BORE* WD6.............31 H4
Centennial Pk *BORE* * WD6 ....31 H4
Century Ct *WATW* * WD18 ....27 F4
Century Pk *WAT* * WD17 ....3 H7
Chaffinch La *WATW* WD18............28 A4
Chalfont La *RKW/CH/CXG* WD3 ...24 A2
Chalk Hl *OXHEY* WD19 ....29 F3
Champions Cl *BORE* WD6.............23 E1
Champneys *OXHEY* * WD19 ....35 F1
Chandler's La
RKW/CH/CXG WD3.....................16 B1
Chandos Rd *BORE* WD6 ....22 C4
Chantry Cl *KGLGY* WD4 ....4 D3
Chapel Cl *GSTN* WD25 ....10 A3
Chapel Wy *ABLGY* WD5 ....6 A1
Chapmans Yd *WAT* WD17................3 H5
Charlock Wy *WATW* WD18............28 A3
Charter Pl *WAT* WD17 ....3 F3
Chartridge *OXHEY* * WD19 ....35 E1
Chartridge Cl *BUSH* WD23 ....30 B3
Chartwell Rd *NTHWD* HA6............34 A5
The Chase *RAD* WD7 ....13 E4
WATW WD18 ....27 H1
Chatsworth Cl *BORE* WD6............22 D5
Chenies Rd *RKW/CH/CXG* WD3 ...14 C4
Chenies Wy *WATW* WD18.............27 H4
Chequers La *GSTN* WD25 ....6 C4
Cherry Cft *RKW/CH/CXG* WD3 .....27 G3
Cherrydale *WATW* WD18 ....2 A5
Cherry Hl *RKW/CH/CXG* WD3 ....15 C5
Cherry Hills *OXHEY* WD19 ....35 F4
Cherry Hollow *ABLGY* WD5.............6 A5
Cherry Tree La
RKW/CH/CXG WD3.....................24 B5
Cherry Tree Rd *WATN* WD24.........10 C5
Cherry Wk *RKW/CH/CXG* WD3 .....15 H4
Cherwell Cl *RKW/CH/CXG* WD3 ...26 D2
Chesham Wy *WATW* WD18............27 H3
Chess Cl *RKW/CH/CXG* WD3 ....26 A1
Chess Hl *RKW/CH/CXG* WD3 ....26 A1
Chess La *RKW/CH/CXG* WD3 ....26 A1
Chess Vale Ri *RKW/CH/CXG* WD3...26 A1
Chess Wy *RKW/CH/CXG* WD3 ......15 G3
Chesswood Ct
RKW/CH/CXG * WD3 ....26 A5
Chester Rd *BORE* WD6 ....23 F5
WATW WD18 ....2 C6
Chestnut Av *RKW/CH/CXG* WD3 ...25 F2
Chestnut Ri *BUSH* WD23 ....30 A4
Chestnut Wk *WATN* WD24............18 B4
Cheviot Cl *BUSH* WD23 ....30 B3

Cheyne Ct *BUSH* * WD23..............29 F1
Chichester Wy *GSTN* WD25 ....11 F2
Chilcott Rd *WATN* WD24 ....9 H5
Chiltern Av *BUSH* WD23 ....30 B3
Chiltern Cl *BORE* WD6 ....22 C4
BUSH WD23..................................30 A3
Chiltern Dr *RKW/CH/CXG* WD3.....25 E4
Chiltern Est *WATN* * WD24 ....18 D3
Chilwell Gdns *OXHEY* WD19 ....34 D3
Chipperfield Rd *KGLGY* WD4 ....4 A4
Chiswell St *WATN* WD24...............18 D2
Chorleywood Bottom
RKW/CH/CXG WD3.....................24 C2
Chorleywood Cl
RKW/CH/CXG WD3.....................26 A4
Chorleywood Rd
RKW/CH/CXG WD3.....................25 G2
Christchurch Crs *RAD* WD7 ....13 F5
Church Cl *RAD* WD7 ....13 F5
Church Farm Wy *GSTN* WD25 ......20 A2
Church Flds *RAD* * WD7 ....13 F5
Church La *GSTN* WD25..................20 A2
KGLGY WD4 ....4 D4
RKW/CH/CXG WD3......................15 F1
Church Rd *WAT* WD17 ....18 B3
Church St *RKW/CH/CXG* WD3......26 B5
WATW WD18 ....3 G4
Church Wk *BUSH* WD23 ....29 H3
Clapgate Rd *BUSH* WD23 ....30 A3
Clare Cl *BORE* WD6 ....32 C3
Claremont Crs
RKW/CH/CXG WD3.....................27 F2
Claremont House *WATW* * WD18...27 F3
Clarence Cl *BUSH* WD23 ....31 E4
Clarendon Ms *BORE* * WD6 ....22 D5
Clarendon Rd *BORE* WD6 ....22 D5
WAT WD17 ....3 F2
Clarke Gn *GSTN* WD25 ....10 B4
Clarke Wy *GSTN* WD25 ....10 B4
Clarkfield *RKW/CH/CXG* WD3.......25 F5
Clarks Md *BUSH* WD23 ....30 B4
Claybury *BUSH* WD23 ....30 A4
Clay La *BUSH* WD23 ....30 A4
Clements Rd *RKW/CH/CXG* WD3...24 C2
Cleveland Crs *BORE* WD6.............33 F2
Clifton Rd *WATW* WD18 ....3 F6
Clifton Wy *BORE* WD6 ....22 D3
The Climb *RKW/CH/CXG* WD3......25 G3
Clitheroe Gdns *OXHEY* WD19......35 E2
Clive Wy *WATN* WD24 ....18 D3
Clockhouse Ms
RKW/CH/CXG * WD3 ....14 D5
The Cloisters *RKW/CH/CXG* WD3...26 B4
Clonard Wy *PIN* HA5.....................35 H5
The Close *BUSH* * WD23 ....29 H3
RAD WD7 ....13 E2
Clover Cl *BORE* WD6 ....23 G5
The Clover Fld *BUSH* WD23 ....29 G3
The Clump *RKW/CH/CXG* WD3.....25 F2
Clydesdale *BORE* WD6 ....33 G2
Clydesdale Pth *BORE* * WD6 ....33 G2
Clyston Rd *WATW* WD18 ....28 A3
Coates Dell *GSTN* WD25...............11 F4
Coates Rd *BORE* WD6 ....32 A4
Coates Wy *GSTN* WD25 ....11 G4
Cobb Gn *GSTN* WD25 ....10 C1
Cob Cl *BORE* WD6.........................33 F2
Cobden Hl *RAD* WD7.....................13 G5
Colburn Av *PIN* HA5......................35 F5
Coldharbour La *BUSH* WD23 ....30 A3
Cole Rd *WAT* WD17.......................18 C3
Coles Gn *BUSH* WD23 ....30 B5
College Rd *ABLGY* WD5 ....6 B5
Colley Land *RKW/CH/CXG* WD3 ...24 C2
Colne Av *OXHEY* WD19 ....28 C3
Colne Ldg *BUSH* * WD23 ....3 K4
Colne Way Ct *WATN* * WD24 ....19 E1
Colonial Wy *WATN* WD24 ....18 D3
Combe Rd *WATW* WD18 ....28 A3
Comet Cl *GSTN* WD25 ....10 A3
The Common
RKW/CH/CXG * WD3 ....24 D2
Common Gate Rd
RKW/CH/CXG WD3.....................24 C2
Common La *GSTN* WD25 ....20 D2
KGLGY WD4 ....4 C2
Common Rd
RKW/CH/CXG WD3.....................24 C1
Compton Pl *OXHEY* WD19 ....35 F3
Comyne Rd *WATN* WD24 ....10 A5
The Comyns *BUSH* WD23 ....30 B5
The Conifers *OXHEY* WD19 ....35 E4
Coningesby Dr *WAT* WD17 ....17 H3
Coningsby Ct *RAD* * WD7 ....13 F5
Coniston Rd *KGLGY* WD4...............4 C2

Connemara Cl *BORE* * WD6 ....33 F3
Cooks Md *BUSH* WD23 ....30 A3
Coombe Hill Rd
RKW/CH/CXG WD3.....................25 F4
Coombe Rd *BUSH* WD23 ....30 B4
Coopers Crs *BORE* WD6 ....23 F5
Copmans Wick
RKW/CH/CXG WD3.....................24 C2
The Coppice *OXHEY* WD19 ....28 D3
Copsewood Rd *WATN* WD24 ....18 C3
Copthorne Cl *RKW/CH/CXG* WD3...26 C2
Copthorne Rd
RKW/CH/CXG WD3.....................26 C3
Corfe Cl *BORE* WD6 ....23 G5
Cornfield Rd *BUSH* WD23 ....30 A1
Cotswold Av *BUSH* WD23 ....30 B3
Cottage Cl *RKW/CH/CXG* WD3 ....26 C3
WAT WD17 ....18 A4
Courtlands Cl *WATN* WD24............9 H4
Courtlands Dr *WAT* WD17 ....9 H5
The Courtway *OXHEY* WD19 ....35 F1
The Courtyards *WATW* * WD18......27 E3
Cow La *BUSH* * WD23 ....29 H3
GSTN WD25 ....10 D5
Cowley Hl *BORE* WD6 ....22 D1
Cowper Ct *WATN* WD24 ....18 B1
Crab La *GSTN* WD25......................12 A3
Crabtree Cl *BUSH* WD23 ....30 A2
Cragg Av *RAD* WD7 ....13 E5
Craig Mt *RAD* WD7 ....13 G4
Craigweil Av *RAD* WD7 ....13 G4
Crakers Md *WATW* * WD18 ....2 E3
Cranefield Dr *GSTN* WD25............11 F1
Cranes Wy *BORE* WD6..................33 F2
The Crescent *ABLGY* WD5...............6 A4
GSTN WD25 ....20 A2
LCOL/BKTW AL2 ....27 H4
RKW/CH/CXG WD3......................27 E3
WATW WD18 ....3 G5
Cress End *RKW/CH/CXG* WD3......25 F5
Croft Ct *BORE* WD6 ....23 G5
Cromer Rd *WATN* WD24 ....18 D2
Cromwell Rd *BORE* WD6..............22 B3
Crossmead *OXHEY* WD19 ....28 C3
The Crosspath *RAD* WD7 ....13 F4
Cross Rd *BUSH* WD23 ....29 F3
Cross St *WAT* WD17 ....3 G2
Crowborough Pth *OXHEY* WD19...35 E3
Crown Ri *GSTN* WD25 ....10 D3
Crown Rd *BORE* WD6 ....22 D3
Croxdale Rd *BORE* WD6 ....22 C4
Croxley Vw *WATW* WD18 ....27 H3
Crusader Wy *WATW* WD18 ....28 A3
Cuffley Av *GSTN* WD25 ....11 E3
Cullera Cl *NTHWD* HA6.................34 A5
Culverden Rd *OXHEY* WD19.........34 C2
Curtis Cl *RKW/CH/CXG* WD3 ....25 F5
Cygnet Cl *BORE* WD6....................23 F3
Cypress Wk *GSTN* * WD25............10 C4

D

Dacre Gdns *BORE* WD6 ....33 G2
Dagger La *BORE* WD6 ....31 F3
Dairy Wy *ABLGY* WD5 ....6 A3
Dale Ct *GSTN* * WD25....................10 B2
Dales Pth *BORE* * WD6 ....33 G2
Dales Rd *BORE* WD6 ....33 G2
Danziger Wy *BORE* WD6...............23 F3
Darrington Rd *BORE* WD6 ....22 B3
Darwin Gdns *OXHEY* WD19..........34 D4
Davenham Av *NTHWD* HA6...........34 A3
Deacons Cl *BORE* WD6 ....32 D1
Deacons Hts *BORE* WD6...............32 D3
Deacons Hill *OXHEY* WD19 ....28 D3
Deacon's Hill Rd *BORE* WD6 ....32 C2
Deakin Cl *WATW* WD18 ....27 H4
Dean Ct *GSTN* * WD25 ....11 E2
Deans *ABLGY* WD5 ....9 G1
De Havilland Wy *ABLGY* WD5.......10 A1
Delamere Rd *BORE* WD6 ....23 E3
Delius Ct *WAT* WD17......................18 B4
Dellfield Cl *RAD* WD7 ....12 D3
WAT WD17 ....18 B4
Dellmeadow *ABLGY* WD5 ....5 H4
Dell Rd *WATN* WD24 ....18 B1
Dell Side *WATN* WD24 ....18 A1
The Dell *RAD* WD7 ....13 F5
Dellwood Ct *RKW/CH/CXG* WD3...25 G5
Delta Gain *OXHEY* WD19 ....35 E1
Denewood Cl *WAT* WD17 ....18 A1
Denham Wy *BORE* WD6 ....23 F3
Denham Wy (North Orbital Rd)
RKW/CH/CXG WD3.....................24 D3
Denmark St *WAT* WD17 ....2 E1
Derby Rd *WAT* WD17 ....3 H4

Derwent Av *PIN* HA5.....................35
Desmond Rd *WATN* WD24 10
Devereux Dr *WAT* WD17 17
De Vere Wk *WAT* WD17 19
Devon Rd *WATN* WD24 19
Dharam Marg *GSTN* * WD25.........20
Diamond Rd *WATN* WD24 18
Dickinson Av *RKW/CH/CXG* WD3...27
Dickinson Sq *RKW/CH/CXG* WD3...27
Digswell Cl *BORE* WD6 22
Dog Kennel La
RKW/CH/CXG WD3.....................24
Doncaster Gn *OXHEY* WD19 34
Dorchester Ct
RKW/CH/CXG * WD3 27
Dorrofield Cl *RKW/CH/CXG* WD3...27
Douglas Av *WATN* WD24 19
Dove Pk *RKW/CH/CXG* WD3 27
Dover Wy *RKW/CH/CXG* WD3.......27
Dowding Wy *GSTN* WD25 10
Downalong *BUSH* WD23................30
Dowry Wk *WAT* WD17 18
Drayton Rd *BORE* WD6 30
The Drive *RAD* WD7 13
RKW/CH/CXG WD3......................14
WAT WD17 18
Dugdales *RKW/CH/CXG* WD3 24
Duke St *WAT* WD17 18
Dulwich Wy *RKW/CH/CXG* WD3...27
Dumfries Cl *OXHEY* WD19............34
Duncan Wy *BUSH* WD23 31
Dunnock Cl *BORE* WD6 23
Dunsmore *OXHEY* * WD19 35
Dunsmore Wy *BUSH* WD23 30
Dunsmore Wy *BUSH* WD23 30
Dunster Ct *BORE* WD6..................23
Durban Rd East *WATW* WD18 28
Durban Rd West *WATW* WD18 28
Durham Rd *BORE* WD6..................22
Durrants Dr *RKW/CH/CXG* WD3...14
Dwight Rd *WATW* WD18 27
Dylan Cl *BORE* * WD6....................33

E

Ealing Cl *BORE* WD6......................23
Earl St *WAT* WD17 3
Eastbury Ct *OXHEY* * WD19 34
Eastbury Rd *OXHEY* WD19 34
East Dr *GSTN* WD25 11
Eastfield Av *WATN* WD24 19
East La *ABLGY* WD5 9
Eastlea Av *GSTN* WD25 11
Easton Gdns *BORE* WD6 33
Ebury Ap *RKW/CH/CXG* WD3 25
Ebury Rd *RKW/CH/CXG* WD3 25
WAT WD17 3
Edgwarebury La *BORE* WD6 32
Edinburgh Av
RKW/CH/CXG WD3.....................24
Edinburgh Dr *GSTN* WD25 11
Edridge Cl *BUSH* WD23 29
Edulf Rd *BORE* WD6 22
Edward Amey Cl *GSTN* WD25.......11
Edward Cl *ABLGY* WD5 9
Elderberry Wy *GSTN* WD25 11
Eldon Av *BORE* WD6 32
Elfrida Rd *WATW* WD18.................27
Elgar Cl *BORE* WD6.......................23
Elgood Av *NTHWD* HA6.................34
Ellenbrook Cl *WATN* * WD24.........19
Ellesborough Cl *OXHEY* WD19 35
Ellwood Gdns *GSTN* WD25 11
Elm Av *OXHEY* WD19 28
Elmcote Wy *RKW/CH/CXG* WD3...25
Elm Ct *WAT* * WD17.......................18
Elm Gv *WATN* WD24......................18
Elmhurst Cl *BUSH* WD23 29
The Elms *BORE* * WD6 32
Elm Tree Wk
RKW/CH/CXG * WD3 24
Elm Wk *RAD* WD7 13
Elm Wy *RKW/CH/CXG* WD3..........27
Elmwood Av *BORE* WD6 23
Elstree Ga *BORE* * WD6 32
Elstree Hl North *BORE* WD6..........32
Elstree Hl South *BORE* WD6..........32
Elstree Pk *MLHL* * NW7 32
Elstree Rd *BUSH* WD23 30
Elstree Wy *BORE* WD6 23
Elton Pk *WAT* WD17 18
Ely Gdns *BORE* WD6 23
Embleton Pl *OXHEY* WD19 35
Enid Cl *LCOL/BKTW* AL2...............27
Essex La *ABLGY* WD5 10
Essex Rd *BORE* WD6 23

T WD17 ...2 D1
urt Rd *WAT* WD17 ...3 G3
n Av WD18 ...2 B7
s Av *GSTN* WD25 ...10 A4
's CI *RKW/CH/CXG* WD3 ...26 D2
syde *WATW* WD18 ...27 F3
ett CI *BUSH* WD23 ...30 D5
ange Rd *WATW* WD18 ...3 F5
er CI *WATN* WD24 ...18 D4
rer Dr *WATW* WD18 ...28 A3

F

ots CI *RAD* WD7 ...13 H4
urn CI *BORE* WD6 ...22 D3
WD23 ...30 A4
eld Av *OXHEY* WD19 ...34 D2
ld CI *RAD* * WD7 ...20 D1
olds *GSTN* WD25 ...11 F4
aven Crs *OXHEY* WD19 ...34 B2
olme Ct *PIN* * HA5 ...35 H5
wns *WAT* WD17 ...18 A3
ed *WATW* WD17 ...9 H5
ay Av *BORE* WD6 ...23 E4
airway *ABLGY* WD5 ...9 G1
field *BUSH* * WD23 ...29 F3
ner Rd *BUSH* WD23 ...29 H3
n Wy *GSTN* WD25 ...11 F3
k Gdns *OXHEY* WD19 ...35 E4
ay CI *WATW* WD18 ...27 G3
CI *BORE* WD6 ...22 B2
ers CI *GSTN* WD25 ...10 C2
La *RKW/CH/CXG* WD3 ...15 G5
BUSH WD23 ...30 A1
ine Rd *WATW* WD18 ...3 F5
nt Wy *BORE* WD6 ...22 B3
rs Wy *BORE* WD6 ...33 G3
n *ABLGY* WD5 ...9 G1
ey Md *RKW/CH/CXG* WD3 ...25 F5
ley St *WATW* WD18 ...3 E3
erstone Gdns *BORE* WD6 ...33 G1
al Wy *WATN* WD24 ...18 D3
n CI *GSTN* WD25 ...11 E3
a CI *BORE* * WD6 ...22 B2
n CI *BORE* * WD6 ...22 B2
e *LCOL/BKTW* AL2 ...7 C5
own Rd *OXHEY* WD19 ...34 D2
lls *ABLGY* WD5 ...9 G3
ly *GSTN* WD25 ...10 C4
ls CI *OXHEY* WD19 ...34 D4
Pl *BUSH* WD23 ...30 A3
nd CI *OXHEY* WD19 ...29 F4
d *OXHEY* WD19 ...34 D3
View Ri *LCOL/BKTW* AL2 ...7 F3
ry *RKW/CH/CXG* WD3 ...25 G5
v *GSTN* WD25 ...11 E4
n *RKW/CH/CXG* WD3 ...25 C5
La *BUSH* WD23 ...29 H1
k * WD18 ...2 B7
k Dr *OXHEY* WD19 ...29 F4
CI *KGLGY* WD4 ...4 D3
e Ct *BORE* WD6 ...32 C1
n CI *RKW/CH/CXG* WD3 ...16 D1
CI *KGLGY* WD4 ...4 D3
s CI *BUSH* WD23 ...3 K2
cres *KGLGY* WD4 ...4 C3
cres Av *LCOL/BKTW* AL2 ...7 G3
s CI *OXHEY* WD19 ...35 G1
ood Wy *OXHEY* WD19 ...34 D3
ce CI *GSTN* WD25 ...10 D4
Dr *ABLGY* WD5 ...6 A5
I *RAD* WD7 ...13 E5
athway *RAD* WD7 ...13 E4
s CI *BUSH* WD23 ...30 B1
eld *LCOL/BKTW* AL2 ...7 H1
Rd *GSTN* WD25 ...10 C2
Wk *BUSH* WD23 ...19 G3
e La *BORE* WD6 ...32 A3
Av *GSTN* WD25 ...11 E4
ur Tubs *BUSH* WD23 ...33 G3
BORE WD6 ...32 A3
WD23 ...30 A2
nd CI *NTHWD* HA6 ...34 A5
ave Pth *OXHEY* WD19 ...35 E4
WD24 ...10 B5
ds CI *GSTN* WD25 ...10 A3
s *OXHEY* WD19 ...35 F2
s Rd *WATW* WD18 ...2 E4
and CI *RKW/CH/CXG* WD3 ...26 D4
and Rd
/CH/CXG WD3 ...27 E3
n Rd *WAT* WD17 ...3 F1
Vy *BUSH* WD23 ...19 G3
Y WD4 ...4 D1
CI *OXHEY* WD19 ...34 C1
ood Av *NTHWD* HA6 ...34 A5

Frobisher CI *BUSH* WD23 ...29 H3
Fulford Gv *OXHEY* WD19 ...34 C1
Fuller Gdns *WATN* WD24 ...18 C1
Fuller Rd *WATN* WD24 ...18 C1
Fuller Wy *RKW/CH/CXG* WD3 ...26 D2
Furtherfield *ABLGY* WD5 ...9 H1
Furze CI *OXHEY* WD19 ...34 D4
Furzehill Pde *BORE* * WD6 ...32 D1
Furzehill Rd *BORE* WD6 ...33 F2
Furze Vw *RKW/CH/CXG* WD3 ...24 B3

G

Gable CI *ABLGY* WD5 ...9 H1
Gables Av *BORE* WD6 ...22 C5
Gaddesden Crs *GSTN* WD25 ...11 E3
Gade Av *WATW* WD18 ...27 H1
Gade Bank *RKW/CH/CXG* WD3 ...27 G1
Gade CI *WATW* WD18 ...27 H1
Gadeside *GSTN* WD25 ...9 H4
Gade Valley CI *KGLGY* WD4 ...4 D2
Gade View Gdns *ABLGY* WD5 ...9 F1
Gadswell CI *GSTN* WD25 ...11 F5
Gallows HI *KGLGY* WD4 ...5 F5
Gallows Hill La *ABLGY* WD5 ...5 F5
Gammons La *WATN* WD24 ...18 B1
Ganders Ash *GSTN* WD25 ...10 B2
Gandhi Ct *WATN* WD24 ...19 E4
Ganton Wk *OXHEY* * WD19 ...35 F3
Garden CI *WAT* WD17 ...2 A1
Garden Rd *ABLGY* WD5 ...5 H5
The Gardens *WAT* WD17 ...18 A4
Garfield St *WATN* WD24 ...18 C2
Garnett Ct *WATN* WD24 ...11 E5
Garnett Dr *LCOL/BKTW* AL2 ...7 G3
Garratts Rd *BUSH* WD23 ...30 B4
Garsmouth Wy *GSTN* WD25 ...11 E5
Garston Crs *GSTN* WD25 ...10 D3
Garston Dr *GSTN* WD25 ...10 D3
Garston La *GSTN* WD25 ...11 E3
The Garth *ABLGY* WD5 ...9 G2
Gartlet Rd *WAT* WD17 ...3 F2
Gate CI *BORE* WD6 ...23 F5
Gateshead Rd *BORE* WD6 ...22 C4
Gaumont Ap *WATW* WD18 ...3 F2
Geddes Rd *BUSH* WD23 ...30 B1
Georges Md *BORE* WD6 ...32 B3
George St *WATW* WD18 ...3 G3
Gibbons Ct *BORE* WD6 ...22 B3
Gibbs Couch *OXHEY* WD19 ...35 E2
Gill CI *WATW* WD18 ...27 F3
Gilliat's Gn *RKW/CH/CXG* WD3 ...24 C1
Gills HI *RAD* WD7 ...13 E4
Gills Hill La *RAD* WD7 ...13 E5
Gills Hollow *RAD* WD7 ...13 E5
Girtin Rd *BUSH* WD23 ...30 A1
Girton Wy *OXHEY* WD19 ...27 F2
Gisburne Wy *WATN* WD24 ...18 B1
Gladstone Rd *WAT* WD17 ...3 H3
The Glebe *GSTN* WD25 ...10 D2
   KGLGY WD4 ...4 D3
Glencoe Rd *BUSH* WD23 ...29 H3
Glencorse CI *OXHEY* * WD19 ...35 E3
Gleneagles CI *OXHEY* WD19 ...35 E3
Glenhaven Av *BORE* WD6 ...22 D5
Glen Wy *WAT* WD17 ...17 H2
Goldcrest Wy *BUSH* WD23 ...30 B5
Goldfinch Wy *BORE* WD6 ...32 D1
Golf CI *BUSH* WD23 ...3 K2
Gonville Av *RKW/CH/CXG* WD3 ...27 E3
Goodrich Ct *GSTN* WD25 ...10 A4
Goodwood Av *WATN* WD24 ...9 H4
Goodyers Av *RAD* WD7 ...13 E2
Goosefields *RKW/CH/CXG* WD3 ...25 H5
Goral Md *RKW/CH/CXG* WD3 ...26 A5
Gorle Ct *GSTN* WD25 ...10 B3
Gosforth La *OXHEY* WD19 ...34 B2
Gosforth Pth *OXHEY* WD19 ...34 B2
The Gossamers *GSTN* WD25 ...11 F4
Grace CI *BORE* WD6 ...23 G3
Grandfield Av *WAT* WD17 ...18 A3
Grange CI *WAT* WD17 ...18 B3
Grange La *GSTN* WD25 ...20 C3
Grange Rd *BORE* WD6 ...32 C2
   BUSH WD23 ...29 F2
Grantham Gn *BORE* WD6 ...33 F2
Granville Rd *WATW* WD18 ...3 G5
Grasmere CI *GSTN* WD25 ...10 C1
Grassington CI *LCOL/BKTW* AL2 ...7 H4
Graveley Av *BORE* WD6 ...33 F1
The Graylings *ABLGY* WD5 ...9 H2
Greasy Ct *ABLGY* WD5 ...6 A5
Great Gv *BUSH* WD23 ...30 A1
Greatham Rd *BUSH* WD23 ...3 K3
Great Pk *KGLGY* WD4 ...4 D4
Great Westwood *KGLGY* * WD4 ...8 B4

Greenbank Rd *WAT* WD17 ...9 G5
Greenbury CI *RKW/CH/CXG* WD3 ...14 B5
Greenfield Av *OXHEY* WD19 ...35 F1
Greenhill Crs *WATW* WD18 ...27 H5
Greenhills CI *RKW/CH/CXG* WD3 ...25 G2
Green La *OXHEY* WD19 ...28 D5
   RKW/CH/CXG WD3 ...26 C2
Greenside *BORE* WD6 ...22 D2
Green St *RKW/CH/CXG* WD3 ...14 B4
Greensward *BUSH* WD23 ...30 A3
The Green *RKW/CH/CXG* WD3 ...26 C1
Greenways *ABLGY* WD5 ...5 G5
The Greenway
Greenwood Dr *GSTN* WD25 ...10 C3
Gregson CI *BORE* WD6 ...23 F4
Grenfell CI *BORE* WD6 ...23 F3
Greycaine Rd *WATN* WD24 ...19 E1
Griffon Wy *GSTN* WD25 ...10 A3
Grosvenor Ct
   RKW/CH/CXG * WD3 ...27 G2
Grosvenor Rd *BORE* WD6 ...22 D5
   NTHWD HA6 ...34 A4
   WAT WD17 ...3 H3
Grosvenor Sq *KGLGY* * WD4 ...5 F2
Grove Bank *OXHEY* * WD19 ...29 E5
Grove Crs *RKW/CH/CXG* WD3 ...26 D1
Grove Hall Rd *BUSH* WD23 ...29 F1
Grove Mill La *RKW/CH/CXG* WD3 ...17 F2
Grove Pl *GSTN* * WD25 ...20 A3
Grove Rd *BORE* WD6 ...22 D3
Grover Rd *OXHEY* WD19 ...29 E3
The Grove *RAD* WD7 ...13 F3
   RKW/CH/CXG * WD3 ...26 D1
Grovewood CI
   RKW/CH/CXG WD3 ...24 A1
Gulland CI *BUSH* WD23 ...30 B2
Gullet Wood Rd *GSTN* WD25 ...10 B4
Gwent CI *GSTN* WD25 ...11 E3
Gypsy La *GSTN* WD25 ...9 G3

H

Hackney CI *BORE* WD6 ...33 G2
Haddenham Ct *OXHEY* * WD19 ...35 E2
Haddon CI *BORE* WD6 ...22 D4
Haddon Rd *RKW/CH/CXG* WD3 ...24 B2
Hadley CI *BORE* WD6 ...32 C2
Hagden La *WATW* WD18 ...2 A5
Haggerston Rd *BORE* WD6 ...22 A5
Haines Wy *GSTN* WD25 ...10 B3
Halifax Rd *RKW/CH/CXG* WD3 ...24 B4
Hallam CI *WATN* WD24 ...18 D4
Hall CI *RKW/CH/CXG* WD3 ...25 F5
Hallowes Crs *OXHEY* WD19 ...34 B2
Halsey Pl *WATN* * WD24 ...18 C2
Halsey Rd *WATW* WD18 ...2 E3
Halter CI *BORE* WD6 ...33 G2
Hamilton CI *LCOL/BKTW* AL2 ...7 H4
Hamilton Rd *KGLGY* WD4 ...9 F2
   OXHEY WD19 ...34 C2
Hamilton St *WATW* WD18 ...3 H7
Hamlet CI *LCOL/BKTW* AL2 ...7 G4
Hammer Pde *GSTN* * WD25 ...10 B2
Hampden Wy *WAT* WD17 ...9 H5
Hampermill La *OXHEY* WD19 ...28 B5
Hancock Ct *BORE* WD6 ...23 F3
Handsworth CI *OXHEY* WD19 ...34 B2
Hangar Ruding *OXHEY* WD19 ...35 G2
Hanover Gdns *ABLGY* * WD5 ...6 A4
Harborne CI *OXHEY* WD19 ...34 D4
Harcourt Rd *BUSH* WD23 ...30 B2
Harding CI *GSTN* WD25 ...20 C3
The Harebreaks *WATN* WD24 ...18 B1
Hare Crs *GSTN* WD25 ...10 A2
Harewood *RKW/CH/CXG* WD3 ...25 H2
Harewood Rd *OXHEY* WD19 ...34 D2
Harford Dr *WAT* WD17 ...17 H2
Harlech Rd *ABLGY* WD5 ...6 B5
The Harlequin *WAT* WD17 ...3 H4
Harriet Walker Wy
   RKW/CH/CXG WD3 ...25 E4
Harriet Wy *BUSH* WD23 ...30 C4
Harris Rd *GSTN* WD25 ...10 A2
Harrogate Rd *OXHEY* WD19 ...34 D2
Harrow Wy *OXHEY* WD19 ...35 G2
Hartfield Av *BORE* WD6 ...32 D1
Hartfield CI *BORE* WD6 ...32 D1
Hartforde Rd *BORE* WD6 ...22 D4
Harthall La *KGLGY* WD4 ...5 H2
Harts CI *BUSH* WD23 ...19 H4
Hartspring La *GSTN* WD25 ...19 G4
Harvest End *GSTN* WD25 ...11 E5
Harvest Rd *BUSH* WD23 ...30 A1
Harvey Rd *RKW/CH/CXG* WD3 ...26 D3

Harwoods Rd *WATW* WD18 ...2 C4
Hastings Wy *BUSH* WD23 ...29 F1
   RKW/CH/CXG WD3 ...27 E1
Hatfield Rd *WATN* WD24 ...18 C3
Hatters La *WATW* WD18 ...27 G3
Havelock Rd *KGLGY* WD4 ...4 C2
Haweswater Dr *GSTN* WD25 ...10 D2
Hawkins CI *BORE* WD6 ...23 F4
Hawthorn CI *ABLGY* WD5 ...10 A1
   WAT WD17 ...18 A2
Hawthorne Rd *RAD* WD7 ...13 F3
Hawtrees *RAD* WD7 ...13 E4
Hay CI *BORE* WD6 ...23 F4
Haydon Dell Farm
   BUSH * WD23 ...29 G4
Haydon Rd *OXHEY* WD19 ...29 F3
Hayfield CI *BUSH* WD23 ...30 A1
Hayling Rd *OXHEY* WD19 ...34 A2
Haywood Dr
   RKW/CH/CXG * WD3 ...25 E2
Haywood Pk *RKW/CH/CXG* WD3 ...25 E2
Hazelbury Av *ABLGY* WD5 ...9 F1
Hazelcroft *PIN* HA5 ...35 H5
Hazel Gv *GSTN* WD25 ...10 C4
Hazel Tree Rd *WATN* WD24 ...18 C1
Hazelwood La *ABLGY* WD5 ...9 G1
Hazelwood Rd
   RKW/CH/CXG WD3 ...27 F3
Healey Rd *WATW* WD18 ...28 A3
The Heath *RAD* WD7 ...13 F2
Heathbourne Rd *BUSH* WD23 ...31 E5
Heathdene Mnr *WAT* * WD17 ...18 B4
Heather CI *ABLGY* WD5 ...10 B1
Heather Ri *BUSH* WD23 ...19 G4
Heathfield Rd *BUSH* WD23 ...29 F1
Heath Ldg *BUSH* * WD23 ...30 C5
Heath Rd *OXHEY* WD19 ...29 E4
Heckford CI *WATW* WD18 ...27 F3
Helston Pl *ABLGY* WD5 ...10 A1
Hemingford Rd *WAT* WD17 ...9 H5
Hemming Wy *GSTN* WD25 ...10 B4
Hempstead Rd *KGLGY* WD4 ...4 C1
   WAT WD17 ...9 G5
   WAT WD17 ...18 B3
Henbury Wy *OXHEY* WD19 ...35 E2
Henderson Pl *ABLGY* WD5 ...6 A1
Herga Ct *WAT* WD17 ...18 B4
Heritage Wk
   RKW/CH/CXG * WD3 ...14 D5
Herkomer CI *BUSH* WD23 ...30 A3
Herkomer Rd *BUSH* WD23 ...29 H2
Herne Ct *BUSH* * WD23 ...30 B5
Herne Rd *BUSH* WD23 ...30 A4
Heronsgate Rd
   RKW/CH/CXG WD3 ...24 A3
Heronslea *GSTN* WD25 ...10 D5
Heswell Gn *OXHEY* * WD19 ...34 B2
Heyford Rd *RAD* WD7 ...21 E1
Heysham Dr *OXHEY* WD19 ...34 D4
Hibbert Av *WATN* WD24 ...19 E2
The Hideaway *ABLGY* WD5 ...6 A5
High Acres *ABLGY* WD5 ...9 G1
High Canons *BORE* WD6 ...23 F1
High CI *RKW/CH/CXG* WD3 ...25 H2
High Cross *GSTN* WD25 ...20 C1
High Elms La *GSTN* WD25 ...6 C5
Highfield *KGLGY* WD4 ...4 B2
   OXHEY WD19 ...35 G2
Highfield Rd *BUSH* WD23 ...29 F2
Highfields *KGLGY* * WD4 ...4 B2
   RAD WD7 ...13 E4
Highfield Wy *RKW/CH/CXG* WD3 ...25 F2
High Firs *RAD* WD7 ...13 E4
Highland Dr *BUSH* WD23 ...30 A1
Highlands *OXHEY* WD19 ...28 D5
The Highlands
   RKW/CH/CXG WD3 ...25 C4
High Rd *BUSH* WD23 ...30 C5
   GSTN WD25 ...10 A3
High St *ABLGY* WD5 ...6 A4
   BORE WD6 ...32 A3
   BUSH WD23 ...29 H3
   KGLGY WD4 ...4 B2
   RKW/CH/CXG WD3 ...26 A5
   WATW WD18 ...2 E3
High Vw *RKW/CH/CXG* WD3 ...25 F1
   WATW WD18 ...28 A3
Highwood Av *BUSH* WD23 ...19 G3
Hilberry Ct *BUSH* * WD23 ...30 A4
Hilfield La *GSTN* WD25 ...20 C5
Hillcroft Crs *OXHEY* WD19 ...28 C5
Hill Farm Av *GSTN* WD25 ...10 B2
Hillfield La South *BUSH* WD23 ...30 D3
Hillingdon Rd *GSTN* WD25 ...10 B3
Hillpoint *RKW/CH/CXG* WD3 ...25 H2
Hill Ri *RKW/CH/CXG* WD3 ...25 C4
Hillrise Av *WATN* WD24 ...19 E2
Hillsborough Gn *OXHEY* * WD19 ...34 B2

Hillside Av *BORE* WD6 ....23 F5
Hillside Cl *ABLGY* WD5 ....9 H1
Hillside Crs *OXHEY* WD19 ....29 E3
Hillside Rd *BUSH* WD23 ....29 F2
  RAD WD7 ....13 G4
  RKW/CH/CXG WD3 ....24 B2
Hilltop Rd *KGLGY* WD4 ....5 C1
Hillview Cl *PIN* HA5 ....35 G5
Himalayan Wy *WATW* WD18 ....28 A3
Hindhead Gn *OXHEY* WD19 ....34 D4
Hodges Wy *WATW* WD18 ....28 B3
The Hoe *OXHEY* WD19 ....35 E1
Hogg La *BORE* WD6 ....31 F1
Holland Gdns *GSTN* WD25 ....10 D4
The Hollies *RKW/CH/CXG* WD3 ...14 A2
Holloway La *RKW/CH/CXG* WD3 ...14 A2
Hollybush Cl *OXHEY* WD19 ....28 D4
Hollygrove *BUSH* WD23 ....30 C4
Holmdale Cl *BORE* WD6 ....22 C4
Holme Lea *GSTN* WD25 ....10 D3
Holme Pk *BORE* WD6 ....22 C4
Holm Oak Pk *WATW* * WD18 ....2 C7
Holmside Ri *OXHEY* WD19 ....34 C2
Holt Cl *BORE* WD6 ....32 C1
Holtsmere Cl *GSTN* WD25 ....10 D4
Holywell Rd *WATW* WD18 ....2 D7
Homefield Rd *BUSH* WD23 ....29 H2
  RAD WD7 ....21 E1
  RKW/CH/CXG WD3 ....24 C1
Home Park Mill Link Rd
  KGLGY WD4 ....5 E5
Homestead Rd
  RKW/CH/CXG WD3 ....26 A4
Home Wy *RKW/CH/CXG* WD3.......25 C5
Hope Gn *GSTN* WD25 ....10 B2
Horbeam Cl *BORE* WD6 ....22 D3
Hornbeams *LCOL/BKTW* AL2 ....7 G4
Horseshoe La *GSTN* WD25 ....10 C1
Howard Cl *BUSH* WD23 ....30 D4
  WATN WD24 ....18 B1
Howard Dr *BORE* WD6 ....33 C1
Howland Ct *PIN* * HA5 ....35 H5
Howton Pl *BUSH* WD23 ....30 C5
Hoylake Gdns *OXHEY* WD19 ....35 F5
Hubbards Rd *RKW/CH/CXG* WD3...24 C2
Hudson Cl *WATN* WD24 ....10 A5
Hunter Cl *BORE* WD6 ....33 F2
Huntercrombe Gdns
  OXHEY WD19 ....34 D4
Hunter's La *GSTN* WD25 ....10 A3
Hunters Ride *LCOL/BKTW* AL2 ....7 F4
Hunton Bridge HI *KGLGY* WD4 ....9 F2
Hurricane Wy *GSTN* WD25 ....10 B2
Hyburn Cl *LCOL/BKTW* AL2 ....7 G4
Hyde La *KGLGY* WD4 ....5 E1
Hyde Rd *WAT* WD17 ....2 D2
Hyver HI *MLHL* NW7 ....33 B3

I

Ilkley Rd *OXHEY* WD19 ....35 F5
Imperial Pl *BORE* * WD6 ....23 E5
Imperial Wy *WATN* WD24 ....18 D3
Ivinghoe Cl *GSTN* WD25 ....11 E4
Ivinghoe Rd *BUSH* WD23 ....30 C5
  RKW/CH/CXG WD3 ....25 E4
Ivy Lea *RKW/CH/CXG* * WD3 ......25 F5

J

Jacketts Fld *ABLGY* WD5 ....6 A4
James Cl *BUSH* WD23 ....29 F2
Jellicoe Rd *WATW* WD18 ....28 B3
Jenkins Av *LCOL/BKTW* AL2 ....7 F4
Jordan Cl *GSTN* WD25 ....10 A4
Jordans Rd *RKW/CH/CXG* WD3 ...25 F4
Jordan's Wy *LCOL/BKTW* AL2 ....7 F4
Jubilee Rd *WATN* WD24 ....18 B2
Judge St *WATN* WD24 ....18 C2
Juniper Av *LCOL/BKTW* AL2 ....7 H5
Juniper Gv *WAT* WD17 ....18 B2

K

Katherine Pl *ABLGY* WD5 ....10 B1
Keble Ter *ABLGY* WD5 ....10 A1
Keele Cl *WATN* WD24 ....3 C1
Kelly Cl *BORE* WD6 ....23 C4
Kelmscott Cl *WATW* WD18 ....28 B3
Kelmscott Crs *WATW* WD18 ....2 C7
Kelshall *GSTN* WD25 ....11 F5
Kemp Pl *BUSH* WD23 ....29 H3

Kemprow *GSTN* WD25 ....12 C4
Kendals Cl *RAD* WD7 ....12 D5
Kenford Cl *GSTN* WD25 ....10 C1
Kenilworth Ct *WAT* WD17 ....18 B3
Kenilworth Dr *BORE* WD6 ....23 F5
  RKW/CH/CXG WD3 ....27 E1
Kennedy Cl *PIN* HA5 ....35 G5
Kensington Av *WATW* WD18 ....2 B5
Kensington Wy *BORE* WD6 ....23 G5
Kent Cl *BORE* WD6 ....23 G2
Keston Ms *WAT* WD17 ....18 C4
Kestrel Cl *GSTN* WD25 ....11 F5
The Kestrels *LCOL/BKTW* AL2 .....7 F5
Kilby Cl *GSTN* WD25 ....11 E4
Kilmarnock Rd *OXHEY* WD19 ......35 E3
Kimble Cl *WATW* * WD18 ....27 H3
Kimble Crs *BUSH* WD23 ....30 B4
Kimbolton Gn *BORE* WD6 ....33 F1
Kimpton Pl *GSTN* WD25 ....11 E3
Kindersley Wy *ABLGY* WD5 ....5 F5
King Edward Rd *OXHEY* WD19 ....29 F3
Kingfisher Lure *KGLGY* * WD4 ......5 E5
  RKW/CH/CXG WD3 ....25 G1
King George Av *BUSH* WD23 ....30 A3
King Georges Av *WATW* WD18 ....27 H2
Kings Av *WATW* WD18 ....2 B5
Kings Cl *NTHWD* HA6 ....34 A5
  WATW WD18 ....3 G5
Kings Farm Rd
  RKW/CH/CXG WD3 ....24 C3
Kingsfield Ct *OXHEY* WD19 ....29 E3
Kingsfield Rd *OXHEY* WD19 ....29 E4
Kingsley Av *BORE* WD6 ....22 C4
Kings Meadow *KGLGY* WD4 ....4 D2
King St *WATW* WD18 ....3 G5
Kingsway North Orbital Rd
  GSTN WD25 ....10 B3
Kingswood Rd *GSTN* WD25 ....10 C3
Kings Yd *RKW/CH/CXG* * WD3 ....26 B5
Kirby Cl *NTHWD* HA6 ....34 A5
Kirkcaldy Gn *OXHEY* WD19 ....34 D2
Kitswell Wy *RAD* WD7 ....13 E2
Knebworth Pth *BORE* WD6 ....33 G1
Knowl Wy *BORE* WD6 ....32 B2
Knutsford La *WATN* WD24 ....19 E2
Koh-i-Noor Av *BUSH* WD23 ....29 H5
Kytes Dr *GSTN* WD25 ....11 E2

L

Ladymeadow *HHS/BOV* HP3 ....4 A1
Lady's Cl *WATW* WD18 ....3 F5
Ladywood Cl *RKW/CH/CXG* WD3...15 C5
The Lake *BUSH* WD23 ....30 C5
Lake Vw *KGLGY* * WD4 ....5 E2
Lamb Cl *GSTN* WD25 ....10 D5
Lambert Ct *BUSH* WD23 ....3 K5
Lambourn Cha *RAD* WD7 ....12 D5
Lammas Rd *WATW* WD18 ....3 G7
Lamorna Cl *RAD* WD7 ....13 G3
Lancaster Wy *ABLGY* WD5 ....6 A5
Lancing Wy *RKW/CH/CXG* WD3 ...27 E2
Lands' End *BORE* WD6 ....32 A3
Lane Gdns *BUSH* WD23 ....30 D5
Langdale Ter *BORE* * WD6 ....23 G5
Langholme *BUSH* WD23 ....30 B5
Langleybury La *KGLGY* WD4 ....9 E3
  WAT WD17 ....17 E1
Langley Crs *KGLGY* WD4 ....4 D4
Langley HI *KGLGY* WD4 ....4 D3
Langley Hill Cl *KGLGY* WD4 ....4 D3
Langley La *ABLGY* WD5 ....6 A5
Langley Lodge La *KGLGY* WD4 .....4 A5
Langley Rd *ABLGY* WD5 ....5 H5
  WAT WD17 ....18 A3
Langley Wy *WAT* WD17 ....18 A3
Langmead Dr *BUSH* WD23 ....30 C5
Langwood Gdns *WAT* WD17 ....18 B3
Lapwing Pl *GSTN* * WD25 ....10 D1
Lapwing Wy *ABLGY* WD5 ....6 B5
Larch Av *LCOL/BKTW* AL2 ....7 F4
The Larches *BUSH* WD23 ....29 F2
Larken Cl *BUSH* WD23 ....30 B5
Larken Dr *BUSH* WD23 ....30 B5
Latimer Cl *WATW* WD18 ....27 H4
Latimer Rd *RKW/CH/CXG* WD3 ...14 A1
Lauderdale Rd *ABLGY* WD5 ....9 F2
Lavinia Av *GSTN* WD25 ....10 D3
Lavrock La *RKW/CH/CXG* WD3 ....26 C4
Lawford Av *RKW/CH/CXG* WD3 ...24 B3
Lawford Cl *RKW/CH/CXG* WD3 ....24 B3
Lawrence Ct *OXHEY* * WD19 ....35 E2
Lea Bushes *GSTN* WD25 ....11 F4

Lea Cl *BUSH* WD23 ....30 A2
Leaford Crs *WATN* WD24 ....18 A1
Leander Gdns *GSTN* * WD25 ....19 F1
Lea Rd *WATN* * WD24 ....18 C2
The Leas *BUSH* WD23 ....19 G4
Leavesden Rd *WATN* WD24 ....18 C2
Lebanon Cl *WAT* WD17 ....9 G5
Le Corte Cl *KGLGY* WD4 ....4 C3
Leeming Rd *BORE* WD6 ....22 C3
Leggatts Cl *WATN* WD24 ....10 A5
Leggatts Ri *GSTN* WD25 ....10 B4
Leggatts Wy *WATN* WD24 ....10 B5
Leggatts Wood Av *WATN* WD24 ...10 C5
Leigh Ct *BORE* * WD6 ....23 G4
Leigh Rodd *OXHEY* WD19 ....35 F2
Lemon Field Dr *GSTN* WD25 ....11 F1
Lemsford Ct *BORE* WD6 ....33 F1
Letchmore Rd *RAD* WD7 ....13 F5
Letchworth Cl *OXHEY* WD19 ....35 E4
Leven Cl *OXHEY* * WD19 ....35 E4
Leveret Cl *GSTN* WD25 ....10 B3
Lewes Wy *RKW/CH/CXG* WD3 ....27 E1
Lexington Cl *BORE* WD6 ....22 C5
Lime Cl *OXHEY* WD19 ....29 E4
The Limes *RKW/CH/CXG* * WD3 ..25 H5
Lime Tree Wk *BUSH* WD23 ....30 D5
  RKW/CH/CXG WD3 ....25 G2
Lincoln Ct *BORE* WD6 ....33 G2
Lincoln Dr *OXHEY* WD19 ....34 D2
  RKW/CH/CXG WD3 ....27 E1
Lincoln Wy *RKW/CH/CXG* WD3 ...27 E1
Linden Lea *GSTN* WD25 ....10 B2
Lindiswara Ct
  RKW/CH/CXG * WD3 ....26 D3
Lingfield Wy *WAT* WD17 ....18 A3
Lingmoor Dr *GSTN* WD25 ....10 D3
Link Rd *BUSH* WD23 ....3 J1
Links Dr *BORE* WD6 ....22 C5
  RAD WD7 ....13 E2
Links Wy *RKW/CH/CXG* WD3 ......17 F5
Linnet Cl *BUSH* WD23 ....30 B5
Linnet Rd *ABLGY* WD5 ....6 B5
Linster Gv *BORE* WD6 ....33 F2
Linton Av *BORE* WD6 ....22 C4
Lion Ct *BORE* WD6 ....23 F5
Liphook Rd *OXHEY* WD19 ....35 E3
Little Bushey La *BUSH* WD23 ......19 H5
Little Graylings *ABLGY* WD5 ....9 H2
Little Green La
  RKW/CH/CXG WD3 ....16 C5
Little Gv *BUSH* WD23 ....30 A1
Little Hayes *KGLGY* WD4 ....4 D3
Little HI *RKW/CH/CXG* WD3 ....24 B3
Little How Cft *ABLGY* WD5 ....5 F5
Little Martins *BUSH* WD23 ....30 A2
Little Orchard Cl *ABLGY* WD5 ......5 C5
Little Oxhey La *OXHEY* WD19 ......35 F4
Little Potters *BUSH* WD23 ....30 C4
Liverpool Rd *WATN* WD18 ....3 F6
Loates La *WAT* WD17 ....3 H5
Local Board Rd *WAT* WD17 ....3 J6
Lodge Av *BORE* WD6 ....32 C2
Lodge Dr *RKW/CH/CXG* WD3 ......25 H1
Lodge End *RAD* WD7 ....13 G3
  RKW/CH/CXG WD3 ....27 G1
Lodge Rd *RKW/CH/CXG* WD3 .....27 G1
Lombardy Wy *BORE* WD6 ....22 B3
London Loop *BORE* WD6 ....33 E3
London Rd *BUSH* WD23 ....29 F3
  RKW/CH/CXG WD3 ....26 B5
Long Barn Cl *GSTN* WD25 ....10 B1
Longcliffe Pth *OXHEY* WD19 ....34 B2
Long Cft *OXHEY* WD19 ....28 C4
Long Elms *ABLGY* WD5 ....9 G2
Long Elms Cl *ABLGY* WD5 ....9 G2
Long Fallow *LCOL/BKTW* AL2 ....7 H1
Long La *RKW/CH/CXG* WD3 ....24 B3
Longspring *WATN* WD24 ....18 C1
Loom La *RAD* WD7 ....21 E1
Loom Pl *RAD* WD7 ....13 F5
Lord St *WAT* WD17 ....3 G3
Loudwater Dr
  RKW/CH/CXG WD3 ....25 H1
Loudwater Hts
  RKW/CH/CXG WD3 ....15 G5
Loudwater La
  RKW/CH/CXG WD3 ....25 H2
Loudwater Rdg
  RKW/CH/CXG WD3 ....25 H1
Louvain Wy *GSTN* WD25 ....10 C1
Lovatts *RKW/CH/CXG* WD3 ....26 D1
Love La *ABLGY* WD5 ....6 A4
  KGLGY WD4 ....4 B3
Lower Derby Rd *WAT* WD17 ....3 H5
Lower High St *WAT* WD17 ....3 H5
Lower Paddock Rd
  OXHEY WD19 ....29 F3

Lower Plantation
  RKW/CH/CXG WD3 1
Lower Rd *RKW/CH/CXG* WD3 2
Lower Tail *OXHEY* WD19 3
Lower Tub *BUSH* WD23 3
Lowestoft Rd *WATN* WD24 1
Loweswater Cl *GSTN* WD25 2
Lowson Gv *OXHEY* WD19 3
Lowther Cl *BORE* WD6 3
Ludlow Md *OXHEY* WD19 3
Ludlow Wy *RKW/CH/CXG* WD3 2
Lullington Garth *BORE* * WD6 3
Lundin Wk *OXHEY* * WD19 3
Lych Ga *GSTN* WD25 1
Lye La *LCOL/BKTW* AL2 ....
Lymington Ct *GSTN* * WD25 1
Lyndon Av *PIN* HA5 2
Lynwood Hts *RKW/CH/CXG* WD3...2
Lysander Wy *ABLGY* WD5 1
Lytham Av *OXHEY* WD19 3

M

Mabbutt Cl *LCOL/BKTW* AL2 ....
Macdonnell Gdns *GSTN* WD25 1
Magnaville Rd *BUSH* WD23 3
Magnolia Av *ABLGY* WD5 ....
Magpie Pl *GSTN* * WD25 1
Malborough Rd *WATW* WD18 ....
Malden Flds *BUSH* WD23 ....
Malden Rd *BORE* WD6 2
  WAT WD17 ....
Mallard Rd *ABLGY* WD5 ....
Mallards Ct *OXHEY* * WD19 3
Mallard Wy *GSTN* WD25 3
The Maltings *KGLGY* WD4 ....
Malvern Wy *RKW/CH/CXG* WD3 ...2
Mandela Pl *WATN* WD24 ....
Mandeville Cl *WAT* WD17 ....
Manor Ct *RAD* WD7 2
Manor Dr *LCOL/BKTW* AL2 ....
Manor House Gdns *ABLGY* WD5 ...
Manor Pl *BORE* * WD6 ....
Manor Rd *WAT* WD17 1
Manor Wy *BORE* WD6 2
  RKW/CH/CXG WD3 ....
Maple Cl *BUSH* WD23 ....
Maple Gv *WAT* WD17 ....
Maple Leaf Cl *ABLGY* WD5 ....
Margaret Cl *ABLGY* WD5 ....
Margeholes *OXHEY* WD19 ....
Marian Gdns *GSTN* WD25 ....
Marion Cl *BUSH* WD23 ....
Markeston Gn *OXHEY* WD19 ....
Market Pl *WAT* WD17 ....
Market St *WATW* WD18 ....
Marlins Cl *RKW/CH/CXG* WD3 ......
Marlins Meadow *WATW* WD18 ......
Marlin Sq *ABLGY* WD5 ....
The Marlins *NTHWD* HA6 ....
Marriott Ter *RKW/CH/CXG* WD3 ...
Marsworth Cl *WATW* * WD18 ....
Martins Cl *RAD* WD7 ....
Marwood Cl *KGLGY* WD4 ....
Masefield Av *BORE* WD6 ....
Mason Cl *BORE* WD6 ....
Matlock Crs *OXHEY* WD19 ....
Maude Crs *WATN* WD24 ....
Maxwell Ri *OXHEY* WD19 ....
Maxwell Rd *BORE* WD6 ....
Maycock Gv *NTHWD* HA6 ....
Maydwell Ldg *BORE* WD6 ....
Mayfare *RKW/CH/CXG* WD3 ....
May Gdns *BORE* WD6 ....
Maylands Rd *OXHEY* WD19 ....
Maythorne Cl *WATW* WD18 ....
Maytree Crs *WATN* WD24 ....
Maytrees *RAD* WD7 ....
Meadowbank *KGLGY* WD4 ....
  OXHEY WD19 ....
Meadow Cl *LCOL/BKTW* * AL2 ......
Meadowcroft *BUSH* * WD23 ....
Meadow Rd *BORE* WD6 ....
  BUSH WD23 ....
  GSTN WD25 ....
Meadow Wy *ABLGY* WD5 ....
  KGLGY WD4 ....
  RKW/CH/CXG WD3 ....
Mead Pl *RKW/CH/CXG* WD3 ....
The Meads *LCOL/BKTW* AL2 ....
The Mead *OXHEY* WD19 ....
Mead Wy *BUSH* WD23 ....
Medway Cl *GSTN* WD25 ....
Meeting Aly *WAT* * WD17 ....
Melbourne Rd *BUSH* WD23 ....

ose Av *BORE* WD6 ....33 E2
Mews *WATW* * WD18 ....3 G5
se Pl *WAT* WD17 ....18 A2
orial Rd *WATW* WD18...............2 D3
lip Rd *BUSH* WD23...................30 B3
den Wy *GSTN* WD25.................19 F1
yfield Cl *BORE* WD6..................22 C4
y Hill Mt *BORE* WD23................30 A5
y Hill Rd *BUSH* WD23................30 A5
on Rd *WATW* WD18....................2 E5
opolitan Station Ap
ATW WD18 ....2 A4
efield Wy *BORE* WD6.................22 B2
ile Furlong *BUSH* WD23 ....30 A1
ile Ope *WATN* WD24.................18 C1
leton Rd
N/CH/CXG WD3........................25 F5
n Wy *WATW* WD24...................18 C1
ed Av *BORE* WD6.....................32 D1
TW WD18 ....2 A4
nd Ct *BORE* WD6.....................23 G3
rook Rd *BUSH* WD23................19 G3
nnium Whf
N/CH/CXG WD3........................26 B5
buse La *ABLGY* WD5....................6 B1
a *KGLGY* WD4............................4 D3
orne Cl *RKW/CH/CXG* WD3 .....26 C2
y *BUSH* WD23..........................19 F4
r Cl *GSTN* WD25......................10 C5
r Ct *BUSH* WD23......................30 A4
n Dr *BORE* WD6.......................33 E1
n St *WATN* WD24.....................18 C3
rva Dr *WAT* WD17......................9 H5
ell Cl *ABLGY* WD5.......................6 B5
 Cl *BUSH* WD23.......................30 A2
field Rd *BUSH* WD23................30 A2
eno Rd *WAT* WD17...................18 B3
yhill Ct
N/CH/CXG * WD3....................25 G5
y Hill Rd
N/CH/CXG WD3.......................25 H5
ca Cl *WATN* WD24......................3 J1
smead *BORE* WD6.....................33 F1
swood Gdns *BORE* WD6 ....33 G2
mouth Rd *WAT* WD17................3 F2
acute Rd *BUSH* WD23...............30 D4
ague Hall Pl *BUSH* WD23..........29 H3
Lane Crossing
TW WD18 ....27 F4
town Rd *OXHEY* WD19.............34 D3
Vw *WATW* WD18......................28 B4
an Cl *NTHWD* HA6...................34 A4
an Gdns *GSTN* WD25................20 A2
ngton Rd *WAT* WD17................13 F3
eth Av *BORE* WD6....................22 C2
ster Cl *OXHEY* WD19...............34 D4
mer Cl *BUSH* WD23..................30 A3
Rd *GSTN* WD25.......................10 C5
Side *LCOL/BKTW* AL2.................7 G4
n Rd *BUSH* WD23....................30 B2
t Pleasant La
L/BKTW AL2................................7 H4
ount *RKW/CH/CXG* WD3..........25 H3
tview *NTHWD* HA6....................34 B5
t Vw *RKW/CH/CXG* WD3...........25 H3
eld Cl *OXHEY* * WD19..............34 D4
eld Gn *OXHEY* WD19................34 D3
eld Rd *OXHEY* WD19................34 C3
rry Cl *WAT* WD17.......................9 H5
en Wk *OXHEY* WD19................35 E3
en Gv *WATN* WD24..................18 D2
esly Cl *OXHEY* WD19................34 D3
o Rd *BUSH* WD23....................30 A2
 Av *WATW* WD18.......................3 H7
nden Ct *WATN* * WD24.............18 C1
etts Cl *GSTN* WD25..................11 F2

N

Gn *OXHEY* WD19......................34 B2
Downs *OXHEY* WD19................28 D4
r *BUSH* WD23.........................29 F1
ap *KGLGY* WD4...........................4 D3
t Pl *WAT* WD17........................18 C4
t Rd *WAT* WD17.......................18 C4
t St *WAT* WD17........................18 C4
t Wood Rd *WAT* WD17.............18 A1
I *BORE* WD6............................32 C1
t *WATW* WD18...........................3 G6
e *BORE* WD6............................23 F3
Wy *RKW/CH/CXG* WD3............25 E4
e *BORE* * WD6.........................22 D5
1 Rd *WATN* WD24....................18 D1
Gv *WATN* WD24.......................18 C3

Newark Gn *BORE* WD6 ....23 C5
Newberries Av *RAD* WD7 ....13 G4
Newbiggin Pth *OXHEY* WD19.....34 D3
Newhouse Crs *GSTN* WD25........10 C2
Newland Cl *PIN* HA5.................35 F5
Newlands Av *RAD* WD7.............13 E3
Newlands Wk *GSTN* WD25.........11 E2
Newlyn Cl *LCOL/BKTW* AL2..........7 F4
New Pde *RKW/CH/CXG* * WD3...26 C3
Newport Md *OXHEY* * WD19......35 E3
Newquay Gdns *OXHEY* WD19.....34 C1
New Rd *GSTN* WD25..................20 D3
    RAD WD7............................12 D5
    RKW/CH/CXG WD3...............15 E3
    RKW/CH/CXG WD3...............26 C2
    WAT WD17...........................3 H5
New St *WATW* WD18...................3 H4
Newton Crs *BORE* WD6.............33 F1
Nicholas Cl *WATN* WD24............18 C1
Nicholas Rd *BORE* WD6.............32 C3
Nicholson Dr *BUSH* WD23..........30 B5
Nicoll Wy *BORE* WD6................33 G3
Nightingale Cl *ABLGY* WD5...........6 B5
    RAD WD7............................13 E5
Nightingale Pl
    RKW/CH/CXG WD3...............26 A4
Nightingale Rd *BUSH* WD23.......29 H2
    RKW/CH/CXG WD3...............25 H4
Niven Cl *BORE* WD6..................23 F3
Noke Side *LCOL/BKTW* AL2...........7 H1
Norbury Av *WATN* WD24............18 D3
Norfolk Av *WATN* WD24.............18 D2
Norfolk Gdns *BORE* WD6............33 C1
Norfolk House
    RKW/CH/CXG * WD3.............26 B5
Norfolk Rd *RKW/CH/CXG* WD3...26 B5
Normansfield Cl *BUSH* WD23......30 A4
North Ap *GSTN* WD25................10 B3
Northcourt *RKW/CH/CXG* * WD3..25 F5
Northfield Gdns *WATN* WD24......18 D1
Northfield Rd *BORE* WD6...........23 E3
Northgate Pth *BORE* WD6..........22 C2
North Hl *RKW/CH/CXG* WD3.......24 A4
North Orbital Rd *LCOL/BKTW* AL2..7 H4
North Orbital Rd (St Albans Rd)
    GSTN WD25.........................11 E2
North Riding *LCOL/BKTW* AL2......7 H4
North Rd *RKW/CH/CXG* WD3......24 C2
Northway *RKW/CH/CXG* WD3.....26 A4
North Western Av *GSTN* WD25....10 B4
North Western Avenue
    (Colne Wy) *WATN* WD24.........10 D5
North Western Avenue
    (Elton Wy) *GSTN* WD25..........20 A4
North Western Avenue
    (Gade Side) *KGLGY* WD4.........9 F4
North Western Avenue
    (Otterspool Wy) *GSTN* WD25...19 C2
North Western Avenue
    (Tylers Wy) *BUSH* WD23.........30 B1
North Western Avenue
    (Watford By-Pass) *STAN* HA7...31 F3
Northwick Rd *OXHEY* WD19........34 D3
Norton Cl *BORE* WD6................22 C5
Norwich Wy *RKW/CH/CXG* WD3..17 E5
Nottingham Cl *GSTN* WD25........10 C2
Nottingham Rd
    RKW/CH/CXG WD3...............24 B5
Novello Wy *BORE* WD6..............23 G3
Numbers Farm *KGLGY* * WD4.......5 F3
Nuttfield Cl *RKW/CH/CXG* * WD3.27 E3

O

Oak Av *LCOL/BKTW* AL2...............7 H4
Oakdale Cl *OXHEY* WD19...........34 D3
Oakdale Rd *OXHEY* WD19..........34 D2
Oakdene Rd *WATN* WD24..........10 C3
Oak Farm *BORE* WD6................33 F2
Oakfield *RKW/CH/CXG* WD3.......25 F4
Oakfield Ct *BORE* * WD6............33 E1
Oak Gn *ABLGY* WD5....................9 H1
Oakhurst Pl *WATW* * WD18..........2 A5
Oaklands Av *OXHEY* WD19.........28 C5
Oaklands Ct *WAT* WD17............18 B3
Oakleigh Dr *RKW/CH/CXG* WD3..27 F3
Oakleigh Rd *PIN* HA5................35 H5
Oakmeade *PIN* HA5..................35 H5
Oakridge *LCOL/BKTW* AL2............7 G3
Oakridge Av *RAD* WD7..............13 E2
Oakridge La *GSTN* WD25...........12 D3
Oaks Cl *RAD* WD7.....................13 E4
The Oaks *BORE* * WD6..............22 D3
    OXHEY WD19.......................28 D5
Oak Tree Cl *ABLGY* WD5..............9 G1
Oak Tree Ct *BORE* * WD6...........32 A3

Oakwood Av *BORE* WD6............33 E1
Oakwood Rd *LCOL/BKTW* AL2......7 G3
Oak Yd *WAT* * WD17.................3 G4
Oberon Cl *BORE* WD6................23 F3
Occupation Rd *WATW* WD18.......2 E6
Octavia Ct *WATN* WD24..............3 H1
Odeon Pde *RKW/CH/CXG* * WD3.26 B5
Odessey Rd *BORE* WD6..............23 E3
Old Barn La *RKW/CH/CXG* WD3..26 C2
Old Forge Cl *GSTN* WD25..........10 B2
Old House La *KGLGY* WD4..........8 D4
Old Mill Rd *KGLGY* WD4..............9 F3
Old's Ap *WATW* WD18................27 F5
Old's Cl *WATW* WD18.................27 E5
Old Shire Lane Circular Wk
    ....24 B4
Old Watford Rd *LCOL/BKTW* AL2..7 F4
On the Hill *OXHEY* WD19...........35 F1
Orbital Crs *GSTN* WD25.............10 A4
Orchard *BUSH* WD23.................30 C5
Orchard Av *GSTN* WD25..............6 C5
Orchard Cl *BORE* WD6...............32 C1
    RAD WD7............................20 D1
    RKW/CH/CXG WD3...............14 C5
    WAT WD17..........................18 A4
Orchard Dr *RKW/CH/CXG* WD3...14 B5
    WAT WD17..........................18 A3
The Orchard on the Green
    ....26 C2
The Orchard *KGLGY* WD4............4 D3
Orchard Wy *RKW/CH/CXG* WD3..25 F4
Organ Hall Rd *BORE* WD6..........22 B3
Oriole Cl *ABLGY* WD5..................6 B5
Orion Wy *NTHWD* HA6..............34 A3
Ormskirk Rd *OXHEY* WD19.........35 E3
Orphanage Rd *WAT* WD17..........3 H1
Orwell Ct *WATN* WD24................3 J2
Osborne Rd *WATN* WD24...........18 D2
Osbourne Av *KGLGY* WD4............4 C2
Osprey Cl *GSTN* * WD25............11 F3
Otley Wy *WATN* WD24...............19 E2
Otterspool La *GSTN* WD25.........19 F2
Otterspool Wy *GSTN* WD25........19 G3
Ottoman Ter *WAT* * WD17...........3 H2
Otway Gdns *BUSH* WD23...........30 D4
Oulton Wy *OXHEY* WD19...........35 G3
Oundle Av *BUSH* WD23.............30 B3
Overstream *RKW/CH/CXG* WD3...25 G1
Owens Wy *RKW/CH/CXG* WD3...26 D2
Oxford St *WATW* WD18................2 E6
Oxhey Av *OXHEY* WD19.............29 E4
Oxhey Dr *OXHEY* WD19.............34 C3
Oxhey La *OXHEY* WD19.............29 E4
Oxhey Ridge Cl *OXHEY* WD19....34 B4
Oxhey Rd *OXHEY* WD19.............28 D4

P

Paddock Cl *OXHEY* WD19...........29 F3
Paddock La *BAR* EN5.................33 H1
The Paddocks
    RKW/CH/CXG WD3...............25 E1
Palace Cl *KGLGY* WD4.................4 C4
Palmer Av *BUSH* WD23..............30 A3
Palmers Rd *BORE* WD6..............23 F3
Pankhurst Pl *WATN* WD24...........3 H2
Pankridge *OXHEY* * WD19..........35 E1
Parish Cl *GSTN* WD25................10 D3
Park Av *BUSH* WD23....................3 K2
    RAD WD7............................13 G2
    RKW/CH/CXG WD3...............25 F2
    WATW WD18.........................3 K2
Park Cl *BUSH* WD23.....................3 K2
Park Crs *BORE* WD6..................22 C5
Parker St *WATN* WD24..............18 C3
Parkfield *RKW/CH/CXG* WD3.......25 E1
Parkgate Rd *WATN* WD24..........18 D1
Parklands *BUSH* * WD23............29 H3
Park Rd *BUSH* WD23.................29 H3
    RAD WD7............................13 F4
    RKW/CH/CXG WD3...............26 B4
    WAT WD17..........................18 B3
Parkside *KGLGY* * WD4..............4 D1
    OXHEY WD19.......................28 D3
Parkside Dr *WAT* WD17.............17 H4
Parkside Rd *NTHWD* HA6...........34 A4
Park Ter *GSTN* * WD25..............11 E2
Park View Rd *PIN* HA5..............34 C5
Park Wy *RKW/CH/CXG* WD3.......25 H5
Parnell Cl *ABLGY* WD5.................6 A4
Parpins *KGLGY* * WD4.................4 D3
Parrotts Cl *RKW/CH/CXG* WD3...26 D1
Parsonage Cl *ABLGY* WD5...........5 H4

Parsonage Rd
    RKW/CH/CXG WD3...............26 A4
Partridge Cl *BUSH* * WD23.........30 B5
Pasture Cl *BUSH* WD23..............30 B4
The Pastures *OXHEY* WD19........28 C4
The Pathway *OXHEY* WD19.........29 E5
    RAD WD7............................13 E5
Paynesfield Rd *BUSH* WD23.......31 E4
Peace Drive *WATW* WD18............2 D2
Peace Prospect *WAT* WD17..........2 D2
Pegmire La *GSTN* WD25.............20 B3
The Pelhams *GSTN* WD25...........11 E4
Penman Cl *LCOL/BKTW* AL2.........7 H1
Penn Cl *RKW/CH/CXG* WD3........24 C3
Penne Cl *RAD* WD7...................13 F3
Penn Rd *RKW/CH/CXG* WD3.......25 E5
Penn Wy *RKW/CH/CXG* WD3......24 C3
Penrose Av *OXHEY* WD19...........35 F1
Penscroft Gdns *BORE* WD6.........33 G1
Penta Ct *BORE* * WD6...............32 D1
Pentland Rd *BUSH* WD23...........30 B3
Percheron Rd *BORE* WD6...........33 G3
Percy Rd *WATW* WD18................3 F4
Peregrine Cl *GSTN* WD25...........11 F3
Perivale Gdns *GSTN* WD25.........10 C3
Perry Md *BUSH* WD23................30 B3
Pheasants Wy
    RKW/CH/CXG WD3...............25 G4
Phillimore Ct *RAD* * WD7...........12 D5
Phillimore Pl *RAD* WD7..............12 D5
Phillipers *GSTN* WD25...............11 E5
Phoenix Cl *NTHWD* HA6............34 A3
Pickets Cl *BUSH* WD23..............30 C5
Pilgrim Cl *GSTN* WD25...............11 E2
Piltdown Rd *OXHEY* WD19.........35 E3
Pine Gv *BUSH* WD23.................19 F4
    LCOL/BKTW AL2.....................7 G4
Pinehurst Cl *ABLGY* WD5.............9 H1
The Pines *BORE* WD6................22 C4
Pinewood Cl *BORE* WD6.............23 G3
    WAT WD17..........................18 B3
Pinewood Ldg *BUSH* * WD23......30 C5
Pinfold Rd *BUSH* WD23..............19 G4
Pinner Rd *OXHEY* WD19.............29 E3
Pinto Cl *BORE* * WD6................33 G3
Pioneer Wy *WATW* WD18............28 A3
Pomeroy Crs *WATN* WD24..........10 C5
Popes La *WATN* WD24...............18 C1
Pope's Rd *ABLGY* WD5................5 H5
Poplars Cl *GSTN* WD25...............10 C1
The Poplars *BORE* * WD6...........22 D3
Potters La *BORE* WD6................23 F3
Potter Street Hl *NTHWD* HA6......34 C5
Pound Fld *GSTN* WD25..............10 A4
Powis Ct *BUSH* * WD23..............30 C5
Powys Ct *BORE* WD6.................23 G5
Prestwick Rd *OXHEY* WD19........35 E1
Prestwood *OXHEY* * WD19.........35 F1
Pretoria Rd *WATW* WD18.............2 D5
Primrose Gdns *BUSH* WD23........30 A4
Primrose Hl *KGLGY* WD4..............5 E2
Princes Av *WATW* WD18..............2 B6
Prince St *WAT* WD17...................3 G1
Priory Vw *BUSH* WD23...............30 D4
Pryor Cl *ABLGY* WD5..................10 A1
Purbrock Av *GSTN* WD25...........10 D5
Purcell Cl *BORE* WD6.................22 A3
Purlings Rd *BUSH* WD23............30 A2
Pursley Gdns *BORE* WD6............22 D2
Puttenham Cl *OXHEY* WD19.......34 D2

Q

Queen Mary's Av *WATW* WD18....27 H1
Queens Av *WATW* WD18..............2 B5
Queens Dr *ABLGY* WD5..............10 A1
The Queen's Dr
    RKW/CH/CXG WD3...............25 E3
Queen's Pl *WAT* WD17.................3 H3
Queen's Rd *WAT* WD17................3 G1
Queenswood Crs *GSTN* WD25.....10 B2
Quickley Brow
    RKW/CH/CXG WD3...............24 A3
Quickley La *RKW/CH/CXG* WD3...24 B3
Quickley Ri *RKW/CH/CXG* WD5...24 A3
Quickly Brow
    RKW/CH/CXG WD3...............24 A3
Quickwood Cl
    RKW/CH/CXG WD3...............25 E3

R

Radlett Park Rd *RAD* WD7..........13 G3
Radlett Rd *GSTN* WD25..............20 B2

WATN WD24 ....3 H2
Radnor Hall *BORE * WD6 ....32 B2
Raglan Gdns *OXHEY* WD19 ....28 C5
Railway Ter *KGLGY* WD4 ....4 D1
Rainbow Ct *OXHEY* WD19 ....28 D3
Ralston Wy *OXHEY* WD19 ....35 E1
Ranskill Rd *BORE* WD6 ....22 D3
Ransom Cl *OXHEY* WD19 ....28 D4
Raphael Dr *WATN* WD24 ....3 J1
Rasehill Cl *RKW/CH/CXG* WD3 ....25 H2
Raven Cl *RKW/CH/CXG* WD3 ....25 H4
Ravenscroft *GSTN* WD25 ....11 F4
Ravenswood Pk *NTHWD* HA6 ....34 B5
Raymond Cl *ABLGY* WD5 ....9 G1
The Readings
RKW/CH/CXG WD3 ....15 E5
Rectory La *KGLGY* WD4 ....4 D2
RKW/CH/CXG WD3 ....26 A5
Rectory Rd *RKW/CH/CXG* WD3 ....26 A4
Reddings Av *BUSH* WD23 ....30 A2
The Reddings *BORE* WD6 ....22 B5
Redhall La *RKW/CH/CXG* WD3 .....16 B3
Redheath Cl *GSTN* WD25 ....10 A4
Red Lion Cl *GSTN* WD25 ....20 A1
Red Rd *BORE* WD6 ....22 C5
Redwing Gv *ABLGY* WD5 ....6 B3
Redwood Ri *BORE* WD6 ....22 D1
Reedham Cl *LCOL/BKTW* AL2 ....7 H3
Reeds Crs *WATN* WD24 ....18 D4
Regal Wy *WATN* WD24 ....18 D2
Regent Cl *KGLGY* WD4 ....4 D3
Regents Cl *RAD* WD7 ....13 F3
Regent St *WATN* WD24 ....18 C2
Rendlesham Av *RAD* WD7 ....21 E1
Rendlesham Wy
RKW/CH/CXG WD3 ....24 B3
Repton Wy *RKW/CH/CXG* WD3 ....26 D2
Reston Cl *BORE* WD6 ....22 D2
Retford Cl *BORE* WD6 ....22 D2
Reynard's Wy *LCOL/BKTW* AL2 .....7 G3
Rhodes Wy *WATN* WD24 ....19 E4
Richards Cl *BUSH* WD23 ....30 C4
Richfield Rd *BUSH* WD23 ....30 B4
Richmond Dr *WAT* WD17 ....17 H4
Richmond Wy
RKW/CH/CXG WD3 ....27 F1
Rickmansworth Rd
RKW/CH/CXG WD3 ....14 D5
WATN WD18 ....27 H1
Ridgefield *WAT* WD17 ....17 H1
Ridgehurst Av *GSTN* WD25 ....10 A2
Ridge La *WAT* WD17 ....9 H5
Ridge St *WATN* WD24 ....18 C2
Ridge Wy *RKW/CH/CXG* WD3 ......25 G4
The Ridgeway *RAD* WD7 ....21 E1
WAT WD17 ....17 H1
Ripon Wy *BORE* WD6 ....33 F2
The Rise *BORE* WD6 ....32 C2
Risingholme Cl *BUSH* WD23 ....30 A4
Riverside Cl *KGLGY* WD4 ....5 E3
Riverside Dr *RKW/CH/CXG* WD3 ..26 A5
Riverside Rd *OXHEY* WD19 ....28 C3
Roberts Rd *WATW* WD18 ....3 G6
Robeson Wy *BORE* WD6 ....23 F3
Robin Hood Dr *BUSH* WD23 ....19 G3
Robin Pl *GSTN* WD25 ....10 C1
Robinson Crs *BUSH* WD23 ....30 B5
Rochester Dr *GSTN* WD25 ....10 D1
Rochester Wy
RKW/CH/CXG WD3 ....27 E1
Rockcliffe Av *KGLGY* WD4 ....5 E4
Rockingham Ga *BUSH* WD23 ....30 B3
Rodgers Cl *BORE* WD6 ....32 A3
Roman Gdns *KGLGY* WD4 ....5 E4
Roman Rd *RAD* WD7 ....13 F4
Roman Wk *RAD * WD7 ....13 E5
Romeland *BORE* WD6 ....32 A3
Romilly Dr *OXHEY* WD19 ....35 F3
Rooks Hl *RKW/CH/CXG* WD3 ....25 H1
Rosary Gdns *BUSH* WD23 ....30 D4
Roseberry Ct *WAT* WD17 ....18 B3
Rosebery Rd *BUSH* WD23 ....30 A5
Rosebriar Wk *WATN* WD24 ....10 A5
Rosecroft Dr *WAT* WD17 ....17 H1
Rosedale Cl *LCOL/BKTW* AL2 ....7 F4
Rose Gdns *WATW* WD18 ....2 D7
Rosehill Gdns *ABLGY* WD5 ....9 F1
Rose Lawn *BUSH* WD23 ....30 B5
The Rose Wk *RAD* WD7 ....13 C5
Ross Crs *GSTN* WD25 ....10 B4
Rossington Av *BORE* WD6 ....22 B2
Rosslyn Rd *WATW* WD18 ....2 E3
Ross Wy *NTHWD* HA6 ....34 A3
Rossway Dr *BUSH* WD23 ....30 B2
Rother Cl *GSTN* WD25 ....10 C3
Roughwood Cl *WAT* WD17 ....17 H2
The Roundway *WATW* WD18 ....28 A3

Roundwood *HHS/BOV* HP3 ....4 B1
Rousebarn La
RKW/CH/CXG WD3 ....16 C2
Rowan Cl *LCOL/BKTW* AL2 ....7 H5
Rowlands Av *PIN* HA5 ....35 H5
Rowley Cl *OXHEY* WD19 ....29 F3
Rowley La *BAR* EN5 ....33 H1
BORE WD6 ....23 G3
Royce Gv *GSTN* WD25 ....10 A3
Royston Gv *PIN* HA5 ....35 G5
Royston Park Rd *PIN* HA5 ....35 G5
Rudolph Rd *BUSH* WD23 ....29 H3
Rufford Cl *WAT* WD17 ....18 A1
Rugby Wy *RKW/CH/CXG* WD3 .....27 E2
Rushmore Ct *WATW * WD18 ....27 G3
Rushton Av *GSTN* WD25 ....10 B4
Russell Ct *LCOL/BKTW* AL2 ....7 H4
Russell Crs *GSTN* WD25 ....10 A4
Russell La *WAT* WD17 ....9 G5
Russell Wy *OXHEY* WD19 ....28 C4
Rutherford Cl *BORE* WD6 ....23 F4
Rutherford Wy *BUSH* WD23 ....30 C5
Rutland Pl *BUSH * WD23 ....30 C5
The Rutts *BUSH* WD23 ....30 C5
Ryall Cl *LCOL/BKTW* AL2 ....7 F3
Ryan Ct *OXHEY * WD19 ....29 F4
Ryan Wy *WATN* WD24 ....18 D3
Ryder Cl *BUSH* WD23 ....30 A3

S

Saddlers Cl *BORE * WD6 ....33 G2
WATN HA5 ....35 H4
Saddlers Wk *KGLGY * WD4 ....4 D3
St Albans Rd *GSTN* WD25 ....10 D5
WAT WD17 ....2 E1
WATN WD24 ....18 C1
St Andrews Ct *WAT * WD17 ....18 C3
St Andrews Ter *OXHEY* WD19 ......34 D4
St Annes Cl *OXHEY* WD19 ....34 D3
St Christophers Ct
RKW/CH/CXG WD3 ....24 C1
St Francis Cl *OXHEY* WD19 ....28 C5
St George's Dr *OXHEY* WD19 ....35 F2
St George's Rd *WATN* WD24 ....18 C2
St James Rd *WATW* WD18 ....3 F6
St John's Rd *WAT* WD17 ....3 H1
St Lawrence Cl *ABLGY* WD5 ....5 H4
St Lawrence Wy *LCOL/BKTW* AL2 ...7 G4
St Leonards Cl *BUSH* WD23 ....29 F1
St Martins Cl *OXHEY* WD19 ....34 D3
St Marys Cl *WATW * WD18 ....3 G4
St Mary's Rd *WATW* WD18 ....3 F5
St Marys Ter *BORE * WD6 ....32 A3
St Marys Vw *WATW * WD18 ....3 G5
St Matthews Cl *OXHEY* WD19 ......29 E3
St Michaels Dr *GSTN* WD25 ....10 C2
St Neots Cl *BORE* WD6 ....22 D2
St Nicholas Cl *BORE* WD6 ....32 A3
St Pauls Wy *WATN* WD24 ....3 H1
St Peter's Cl *BUSH* WD23 ....30 C5
St Peters Wy *RKW/CH/CXG* WD3 ..24 A1
St Vincents Cottages
*WATW * WD18 ....3 F4
Salisbury Rd *WATN* WD24 ....18 C2
Salters Cl *RKW/CH/CXG* WD3 ......26 B5
Salters Gdns *WAT * WD17 ....18 B3
Sandown Rd *WATN* WD24 ....18 D2
Sandringham Rd *WATN* WD24 ......18 C1
Sandy La *BUSH* WD23 ....20 B5
NTHWD HA6 ....34 A1
Sandy Ldg *PIN * HA5 ....35 H5
Sarratt La *RKW/CH/CXG* WD3 ......15 G4
Sarratt Rd *RKW/CH/CXG* WD3 .....15 G1
Sawtry Wy *BORE* WD6 ....22 D2
Saxon Ct *BORE* WD6 ....22 B3
Saxton Ms *WAT * WD17 ....18 B3
Scammell Wy *WATW* WD18 ....28 A3
School La *BUSH* WD23 ....30 A4
LCOL/BKTW AL2 ....11 G3
School Md *ABLGY* WD5 ....9 G1
Schubert Rd *BORE* WD6 ....32 A3
Scotscraig *RAD* WD7 ....13 E4
Scots Hill *RKW/CH/CXG* WD3 ......26 C3
Scots Hill Cl *RKW/CH/CXG* WD3 ..26 C3
Scots Mill La *RKW/CH/CXG* WD3 ..26 C3
Scottswood Cl *BUSH* WD23 ....19 F4
Scottswood Rd *BUSH* WD23 ....19 F4
Scotts Sq *RAD* WD7 ....13 F4
Scrubbitts Park Rd *RAD* WD7 ......13 F4
Seabrook Rd *KGLGY* WD4 ....5 G2
Seacroft Gdns *OXHEY* WD19 ....35 E3
Searches La *ABLGY* WD5 ....11 E4
Second Av *GSTN* WD25 ....11 F4
Sequoia Cl *BUSH* WD23 ....30 C5
Seven Acres *NTHWD* HA6 ....34 B5

Severn Wy *GSTN* WD25 ....10 D3
Shackleton Wy *ABLGY * WD5 ....10 B1
Shady Bush Cl *BUSH* WD23 ....30 B4
Shady La *WAT* WD17 ....3 F1
Shaftesbury Ct
*RKW/CH/CXG * WD3 ....27 F2
Shaftesbury Rd *WAT* WD17 ....3 H3
Shakespeare St *WATN* WD24 ......18 C2
Shanklin Gdns *OXHEY* WD19 ....34 D3
Sheepcot Dr *GSTN* WD25 ....10 D3
Sheepcot La *GSTN* WD25 ....10 B2
Shelley Cl *NTHWD* HA6 ....34 A4
Shenley Hl *RAD* WD7 ....13 G3
Shenley Rd *BORE* WD6 ....22 D5
Shenwood Ct *BORE* WD6 ....22 D1
Shepherd's La
RKW/CH/CXG WD3 ....24 C3
Shepherds Rd *WATW* WD18 ....2 B5
Shepherds Wy
RKW/CH/CXG WD3 ....25 G4
Shepperton Cl *BORE* WD6 ....23 G4
Sheppey's La *KGLGY* WD4 ....5 H2
Sheraton Cl *BORE* WD6 ....32 C2
Sheraton Ms *WATW * WD18 ....27 H1
Sherborne Ct
RKW/CH/CXG WD3 ....27 E1
Sheridan Rd *OXHEY* WD19 ....29 E4
Sheriff Wy *GSTN* WD25 ....10 B2
Sherland Ct *RAD * WD7 ....13 H4
Sherwoods Rd *OXHEY* WD19 ......29 F4
Shetland Cl *BORE* WD6 ....33 G3
Shire La *RKW/CH/CXG* WD3 ....24 A2
Shiremeade *BORE* WD6 ....32 C2
Shirley Rd *ABLGY* WD5 ....10 A1
Short La *LCOL/BKTW* AL2 ....7 F3
Sidmouth Cl *OXHEY* WD19 ....34 C1
Silk Mill Rd *OXHEY* WD19 ....28 C4
Silverdale Rd *BUSH* WD23 ....29 F2
Silver Dell *WATN* WD24 ....10 A4
Silver Trees *LCOL/BKTW* AL2 ....7 G4
Sinderby Cl *BORE* WD6 ....22 B3
Sirus Rd *NTHWD* HA6 ....34 B4
Siskin Cl *BORE* WD6 ....32 D1
BUSH WD23 ....29 F1
Sixth Av *GSTN* WD25 ....11 E4
Skidmore Wy
RKW/CH/CXG WD3 ....26 B5
Slade Ct *RAD* WD7 ....13 G5
Sleaford Gn *OXHEY* WD19 ....35 G5
Smith St *WATN* WD18 ....3 G5
Solar Ct *WATW * WD18 ....2 A6
Solesbridge Cl
RKW/CH/CXG WD3 ....15 E2
Solesbridge La
RKW/CH/CXG WD3 ....15 E5
Solomon's Hl
RKW/CH/CXG WD3 ....26 A4
Somers Wy *BUSH* WD23 ....30 B4
Sonia Cl *OXHEY* WD19 ....28 D4
Sotheron Rd *WAT* WD17 ....3 G1
Souldern St *WATW* WD18 ....2 D6
South Cottage Dr
RKW/CH/CXG WD3 ....25 E2
South Cottage Gdns
RKW/CH/CXG WD3 ....25 E2
Southfield Av *WATN* WD24 ....18 D2
South Park Av
RKW/CH/CXG WD3 ....25 E2
South Riding *LCOL/BKTW* AL2 ....7 H4
South Rd *RKW/CH/CXG* WD3 ......24 B2
Southsea Av *WATW* WD18 ....2 C4
South View Rd *PIN* HA5 ....34 C5
South Wy *ABLGY* WD5 ....9 G2
Southwold Rd *WATN* WD24 ....18 D1
Sparrows Herne *BUSH* WD23 ......30 A4
Sparrows Wk *BUSH * WD23 ....30 B4
Sparrows Wick *BUSH * WD23 ....30 B5
Spencer Wk
RKW/CH/CXG WD3 ....25 H2
The Spinney *WAT* WD17 ....18 B3
Spring Cl *BORE* WD6 ....22 B3
Spring Crofts *BUSH* WD23 ....29 H2
Springfield *BUSH* WD23 ....30 C5
Springfield Cl
RKW/CH/CXG WD3 ....27 E2
Springfield Rd *GSTN* WD25 ....10 C2
Spring Gdns *GSTN* WD25 ....10 D4
Spur Cl *ABLGY* WD5 ....9 G2
The Square *WATN* WD24 ....18 C1
The Squirrels *BUSH* WD23 ....30 C5
Stag La *RKW/CH/CXG* WD3 ....24 B3
Stainer Rd *BORE* WD6 ....22 A3
Stamford Rd *WAT* WD17 ....18 C4
Stanborough Av *BORE* WD6 ....22 D2
Stanbury Av *WAT* WD17 ....17 H1
Standfield *ABLGY* WD5 ....5 H5
Stangate Crs *BORE* WD6 ....33 H2
Stanley Gdns *BORE* WD6 ....22 B2

Stanley Rd *WAT* WD17 ....
Stanmore Rd *WATN* WD24 1
Stapleton Rd *BORE* WD6 2
Starling Pl *GSTN * WD25 1
Station Ap *OXHEY* WD19 3
RAD WD7 1
RKW/CH/CXG WD3 2
*WATW * WD18
Station Footpath *KGLGY* WD4 ......
Station Rd *BORE* WD6 3
KGLGY WD4
LCOL/BKTW AL2 ....
RAD WD7 1
RKW/CH/CXG WD3 1
WAT WD17
Steeplands *BUSH* WD23 ....
Stephenson Wy *BUSH* WD23 1
Stevenage Crs *BORE* WD6 2
Stevens Gn *BUSH* WD23 ....
Stewart Cl *ABLGY* WD5 ....
Stilton Pth *BORE* WD6 ....
Stirling Wy *ABLGY* WD5 ....
BORE WD6
Stockport Rd
RKW/CH/CXG WD3 2
Strangeways *WAT* WD17 1
Stratfield Rd *BORE* WD6 ....
Stratford Rd *WAT* WD17 ....
Stratford Wy *LCOL/BKTW* AL2 ....
WAT WD17
Stretton Wy *BORE* WD6 2
Stripling Wy *WATW* WD18............
Stuart Ct *BORE* WD6 ....
Stud Gn *GSTN* WD25 ....
The Studios *BUSH* WD23..............
Studio Wy *BORE* WD6 ....
Suffolk Cl *BORE* WD6...................
Sullivan Wy *BORE* WD6................
Summerfeild Rd *GSTN* WD25 ....
Summer Gv *BORE* WD6................
Summer Hl *BORE* WD6 ....
Summerhouse La *GSTN* WD25 .....
Summerhouse Wy *ABLGY* WD5 .....
Summer Pl *WATW * WD18 ....
Summers Wd *BORE * WD6 3
Sunderland Gv *GSTN* WD25 ....
Sussex Rd *WATN* WD24 ....
Sutcliffe Cl *BUSH* WD23 ....
Sutton Rd *WAT* WD17 ....
Swallow Cl *BUSH* WD23 ....
RKW/CH/CXG WD3
Swallow Oaks *ABLGY* WD5 ....
Swan Cl *RKW/CH/CXG* WD3 ....
Swanston Pth *OXHEY* WD19 ....
Swiss Av *WATW* WD18 ....
Swiss Cl *WATW* WD18...................
Sycamore Ap
RKW/CH/CXG WD3
Sycamore Cl *BUSH* WD23 ....
GSTN WD25
Sycamore Rd
RKW/CH/CXG WD3
The Sycamores *RAD* WD7.............
Sydney Rd *WATW* WD18 ....
Sylvia Av *PIN* HA5 ....

T

Talbot Av *OXHEY* WD19................
Talbot Rd *RKW/CH/CXG* WD3.......
Tallis Wy *BORE* WD6....................
Tanners Hl *ABLGY* WD5 ....
Tanners Wood La *ABLGY* WD5 ......
Tate Gdns *BUSH* WD23 ....
Tauber Cl *BORE* WD6 ....
Tavistock Rd *WATN* WD24............
Telford Cl *GSTN* WD25 ....
Temple Cl *WAT* WD17 ....
Templepan La
RKW/CH/CXG WD3
Tempsford Av *BORE* WD6.............
Tennison Av *BORE* WD6 ....
Terrace Gdns *WAT* WD17 ....
Thellusson Wy
*RKW/CH/CXG * WD3
Thellusson Ct *RAD * WD7 ....
Theobald St *RAD* WD7.................
Third Av *GSTN* WD25 ....
Thirsk Rd *BORE* WD6 ....
Thompson Wy
RKW/CH/CXG WD3
Thorn Av *BUSH* WD23 ....
Thornbury Gdns *BORE* WD6.........
Thornton Gv *PIN* HA5 ....
Thorpe Crs *OXHEY* WD19 ....
Three Valleys Wy *BUSH* WD23......

t Farm La *BORE* WD6 ....23 F4
stle Pl *GSTN* * WD25 ....10 D1
ms *WATN* WD24 ....18 C1
sh Gn *RKW/CH/CXG* WD3 ....25 H4
es Cl *GSTN* WD25 ....11 F4
s Hill Rd *ABLGY* WD5 ....6 A4
ouse Cl *BORE* WD6 ....22 C5
er Rdg *RKW/CH/CXG* WD3 .....25 H1
ell Ms *BORE* WD6 ....33 G2
Barn Ct *ABLGY* * WD5 ....6 A3
h Rd *BUSH* WD23 ....30 D4
ate Cl *RKW/CH/CXG* WD3 .....25 E1
s Cl *WATW* WD18 ....2 A7
ts La *WATW* WD18 ....27 C4
kins Cl *BORE* WD6 ....22 B3
eys Mill Cl *KGLGY* WD4 ....4 D3
orth Rd *BORE* WD6 ....22 C3
rsis Wk *WAT* WD17 ....17 H3
llance Wy *GSTN* WD25 ....10 D2
se Wy *OXHEY* WD19 ....34 D2
nt Rd *GSTN* WD25 ....10 A3
y Hall Cl *WATN* WD24 ....3 H2
n Ldg *BUSH* * WD23 ....29 F1
Ri *RKW/CH/CXG* WD3 ....15 G5
tstream Wy
N/CH/CXG WD3 ....25 G1
ey Ri *ABLGY* WD5 ....5 H5
lers Wy *BUSH* WD23 ....30 D5
r St *WATW* WD18 ....3 G6
Av *WATN* WD24 ....19 E1
Ct *BORE* WD6 ....22 B4
Dr *WATN* WD24 ....19 F2
Manor Gdns *GSTN* WD25 .....11 E1
Wk *WATN* WD24 ....19 E1
Wy *RKW/CH/CXG* WD3 ....25 F5
el Wood Cl *WAT* WD17 ....18 A1
el Wood Rd *WAT* WD17 ....18 A1
erry Ct *OXHEY* * WD19 ....34 D2
erry Dr *LCOL/BKTW* AL2 ....7 F4
r Rd *BUSH* WD23 ....30 B1
ys Orch
W/CH/CXG WD3 ....24 C2
urnstones *GSTN* WD25 ....11 F5
uds Cl *RKW/CH/CXG* WD3 .....26 D2
rd Cl *BORE* * WD6 ....22 B2
Cl *KGLGY* WD4 ....4 C3
field *ABLGY* WD5 ....6 A5

U

rsity Cl *BUSH* WD23 ....29 G1
ds *RKW/CH/CXG* WD3 ....26 C3
olands *LCOL/BKTW* AL2 ....7 F4
Hwy *ABLGY* WD5 ....9 F1
Hill Ri *RKW/CH/CXG* WD3 .....25 G3
Hitch *OXHEY* WD19 ....29 F5
Paddock Rd
EY WD19 ....29 F3
Station Rd *RAD* WD7 ....13 F4
Tail *OXHEY* WD19 ....35 F2
Lodge Cl *BUSH* WD23 ....30 B4
Rd *WATW* WD18 ....2 E4
ge Rd *RKW/CH/CXG* WD3 .....25 G5

V

Vale Av *BORE* WD6 ....33 G2
Valency Cl *NTHWD* HA6 ....34 A3
Vale Rd *BUSH* WD23 ....29 F2
Valley Pk *WATW* * WD18 ....27 F4
Valley Ri *GSTN* WD25 ....10 C2
Valley Rd *RKW/CH/CXG* WD3 .....25 F2
Valley Wk *RKW/CH/CXG* WD3 .....27 F2
Vega Crs *NTHWD* HA6 ....34 A4
Vega Rd *BUSH* WD23 ....30 B4
Vera Ct *OXHEY* WD19 ....29 E4
Ver-Colne Valley Wk *BUSH* WD23 ...3 J3
Verdure Cl *GSTN* WD25 ....11 F1
Vernon Rd *BUSH* WD23 ....29 F2
Vicarage La *KGLGY* WD4 ....4 C3
Vicarage Rd *WATW* WD18 ....2 D7
Victoria Cl *RKW/CH/CXG* WD3 .....26 A4
Victoria Rd *BUSH* WD23 ....30 A5
WATN WD24 ....18 C2
Victor Smith Ct *LCOL/BKTW* * AL2 .....7 H5
Villiers Rd *BUSH* WD23 ....29 F3
Violet Wy *RKW/CH/CXG* WD3 .....25 H1
Vivian Cl *OXHEY* WD19 ....34 B1
Vivian Gdns *OXHEY* WD19 ....28 B5

W

Wadham Rd *ABLGY* WD5 ....6 A5
Wagon Wy *RKW/CH/CXG* WD3 .....15 H5
Walnut Gn *BUSH* WD23 ....19 C4
Walshford Wy *BORE* WD6 ....22 D2
Walton Rd *BUSH* WD23 ....3 K4
Walverns Cl *OXHEY* WD19 ....28 B1
Wansford Pk *BORE* WD6 ....33 G1
Warenford Wy *BORE* WD6 ....22 D3
Warneford Pl *OXHEY* WD19 ....29 F3
Warren Gv *BORE* WD6 ....33 G1
Warren Rd *BUSH* WD23 ....30 B5
The Warren *KGLGY* WD4 ....4 C3
RAD WD7 ....13 F2
Warwick Cl *BUSH* WD23 ....30 D4
Warwick Ct *RKW/CH/CXG* WD3 .....15 E5
Warwick Pl *BORE* * WD6 ....23 C5
Warwick Rd *BORE* WD6 ....23 C5
Warwick Wy *RKW/CH/CXG* WD3 .....27 F1
The Waterfront *BORE* * WD6 ....31 G3
The Watergate *OXHEY* WD19 .....35 F1
Water La *KGLGY* WD4 ....5 E3
WAT WD17 ....3 H5
Waterman Cl *OXHEY* WD19 ....28 C3
Waters Dr *RKW/CH/CXG* WD3 .....26 B5
Waterside *KGLGY* WD4 ....4 D3
RAD WD7 ....13 G3
Waterside Ct *KGLGY* WD4 ....5 E3
Watford Field Rd *WATW* WD18 .....3 H6
Watford Heath *OXHEY* WD19 .....29 E4
Watford Heath Farm
OXHEY * WD19 ....29 E4
Watford Int *WATN* WD24 ....18 D3
Watford Rd *BORE* WD6 ....31 H3
KGLGY WD4 ....4 D4
LCOL/BKTW AL2 ....7 H1
RAD WD7 ....12 D5

RKW/CH/CXG WD3 ....26 D3
Watling Knoll *RAD* WD7 ....13 E2
Wayside Av *BUSH* WD23 ....30 C3
Weall Gn *GSTN* WD25 ....10 C1
Webber Cl *BORE* WD6 ....32 A3
Welbeck Cl *BORE* WD6 ....22 D5
Well End Rd *BORE* WD6 ....23 F1
Wellesley Av *NTHWD* HA6 ....34 A4
Wellington Cl *OXHEY* WD19 ....35 F2
Wellington Rd *WAT* WD17 ....3 F1
Wellstones *WAT* WD17 ....3 F2
Wendover Wy *BUSH* WD23 ....30 B3
Wensum Wy *RKW/CH/CXG* WD3 .....26 A5
Wentbridge Pth *BORE* WD6 ....22 D2
Wentworth Av *BORE* WD6 ....32 C2
Wentworth Cl *WAT* WD17 ....18 A2
Westbury Rd *WATW* WD18 ....3 F6
West Dr *GSTN* WD25 ....10 C5
Westfield Av *WATN* WD24 ....19 E2
Westland Rd *WAT* WD17 ....3 F1
Westlea Av *GSTN* WD25 ....19 F1
West Riding *LCOL/BKTW* AL2 ....7 G4
West St *WAT* WD17 ....18 C4
Westview Ct *BORE* WD6 ....32 A3
West View Gdns *BORE* WD6 ....32 A3
West Wy *RKW/CH/CXG* WD3 ....25 G5
Westwick Pl *GSTN* WD25 ....10 D3
Wetherby Rd *BORE* WD6 ....22 B3
Wharf La *RKW/CH/CXG* WD3 ....26 B4
Wheelright Cl *BUSH* WD23 ....30 A3
Whippendell Rd *WATW* WD18 ....2 D5
WATW WD18 ....27 H2
Whisper Wd
RKW/CH/CXG WD3 ....15 G5
White Craig Cl *PIN* HA5 ....35 H4
Whitegates Cl
RKW/CH/CXG WD3 ....26 D1
Whitehouse Av *BORE* WD6 ....33 E1
Whitelands Av
RKW/CH/CXG WD3 ....14 A5
White Shack La
RKW/CH/CXG WD3 ....16 C1
Whitfield Wy *RKW/CH/CXG* WD3 .....25 E5
Whitlars Dr *KGLGY* WD4 ....4 C2
Whitley Cl *ABLGY* WD5 ....10 B1
Whitwell Rd *GSTN* WD25 ....11 E4
Widgeon Wy *GSTN* WD25 ....11 F5
Wiggenhall Rd *WATW* WD18 ....3 F5
Wilcon Wy *GSTN* WD25 ....11 E3
Wilcot Av *OXHEY* WD19 ....29 F4
Wilcot Cl *OXHEY* WD19 ....29 F4
Wilcox Cl *BORE* WD6 ....22 D2
Wild Oaks Cl *NTHWD* HA6 ....34 A5
Wildwood Av *LCOL/BKTW* AL2 ....7 G4
Williamson Wy
RKW/CH/CXG WD3 ....25 F5
William St *BUSH* WD23 ....3 K3
Williams Wy *RAD* WD7 ....13 H4
Willow Dene *BUSH* WD23 ....30 D4
Willow Edge *KGLGY* WD4 ....4 D3
Willow End *NTHWD* HA6 ....34 B5
Willow La *WATW* WD18 ....2 D7
The Willows *BORE* * WD6 ....22 D3
OXHEY WD19 ....28 C4
Willow Wy *LCOL/BKTW* AL2 ....7 H1
RAD WD7 ....12 D5
Wimborne Gv *WAT* WD17 ....17 H1
Winchester Wy
RKW/CH/CXG WD3 ....27 E2

Winchfield Wy
RKW/CH/CXG WD3 ....25 H4
Windermere Cl
RKW/CH/CXG WD3 ....24 C2
Windmill Dr *RKW/CH/CXG* WD3 .....26 C3
Windmill La *BUSH* WD23 ....30 D5
Windmill St *BUSH* WD23 ....30 D5
Windsor Rd *WATN* WD24 ....18 D2
Windsor Wy *RKW/CH/CXG* WD3 .....25 F5
Wingfield Ct *WATW* * WD18 ....27 G3
Winstre Rd *BORE* WD6 ....22 D3
Winton Ap *RKW/CH/CXG* WD3 .....27 F2
Winton Crs *RKW/CH/CXG* WD3 .....27 E2
Winton Dr *RKW/CH/CXG* WD3 .....27 F2
The Wintons *BUSH* * WD23 ....30 C5
Witney Cl *PIN* HA5 ....35 C5
Woburn Cl *BUSH* WD23 ....30 B3
Woodfield Ri *BUSH* WD23 ....30 C4
Woodfield Rd *RAD* WD7 ....13 F5
Woodfields *WATW* * WD18 ....3 G2
Woodford Rd *WAT* WD17 ....3 G1
Woodgate *GSTN* WD25 ....10 C2
Woodgate Crs *NTHWD* HA6 ....34 B5
Woodhall La *OXHEY* WD19 ....35 E2
Woodhouse Eaves *NTHWD* HA6 .....34 B4
Woodhurst Av *GSTN* WD25 ....11 E4
Woodland Dr *WAT* WD17 ....2 C1
Woodland La *RKW/CH/CXG* WD3 .....14 C5
Woodlands *RAD* WD7 ....13 F3
Woodlands Cl *BORE* WD6 ....33 E1
Woodlands Rd *BUSH* WD23 ....29 F1
KGLGY WD4 ....4 D1
Woodland Wy *ABLGY* WD5 ....6 A1
Woodmans Yd *WAT* WD17 ....3 H5
Woodmere Av *WATN* WD24 ....19 E2
Woodpecker Cl *BUSH* WD23 ....30 B5
Woodshots Meadow
WATW WD18 ....27 G2
Woodside *BORE* WD6 ....32 C1
WATN WD24 ....18 B1
Woodside Rd *GSTN* WD25 ....6 C5
LCOL/BKTW AL2 ....7 G4
The Woods *NTHWD* HA6 ....34 B4
RAD WD7 ....13 G3
Woodstock Rd *BUSH* WD23 ....30 D4
Woodville Court Ms
WAT * WD17 ....18 B4
Woodwaye *OXHEY* WD19 ....28 D4
Woolmer Cl *BORE* WD6 ....22 D2
Woolmerdine Ct *BUSH* WD23 ....3 K3
Wren Crs *BUSH* WD23 ....30 B5
Wyatt Cl *BUSH* WD23 ....30 D4
Wyatt's Cl *RKW/CH/CXG* WD3 .....15 F5
Wyatt's Rd *RKW/CH/CXG* WD3 .....25 E1

Y

Yarmouth Rd *WATN* WD24 ....18 C2
Ye Cnr *BUSH* WD23 ....29 E3
Yew Tree Ct *BORE* WD6 ....32 A3
York Cl *KGLGY* WD4 ....4 D3
York Crs *BORE* WD6 ....23 G4
Yorke Ga *WAT* WD17 ....18 B4
Yorke Rd *RKW/CH/CXG* WD3 .....26 D3
York Rd *WATW* WD18 ....3 H7
York Wy *GSTN* WD25 ....11 E5
Yule Cl *LCOL/BKTW* AL2 ....7 G4

Index - featured places

s Langley Primary School
GY WD5 ....5 H3
swood Medical Centre
...............10 B1
Wood Infant School
N WD25 ....10 C2
Wood Junior School
N WD25 ....10 C2
am Country Park
E WD6 ....31 G2
am Golf & Country Club
N WD25 ....20 A2
am School
E WD6 ....21 E4
Hills Primary School
/CH/CXG WD3 ....25 F3
d Junior School
...............30 A4
nd JMI School
GY WD5 ....6 A2
eld Junior Middle &
nt School
...............18 B1

Berkeley Clinic
RKW/CH/CXG WD3 ....25 H5
Borehamwood FC
BORE WD6 ....23 E4
Borehamwood Industrial Park
BORE WD6 ....23 G4
Boulevard 25 Retail Park
BORE WD6 ....22 D5
Bournehall J & I School
BUSH WD23 ....29 H2
Breakspeare School
ABLGY WD5 ....5 H5
Bromet Primary School
OXHEY WD19 ....29 E4
Bushey Golf & Country Club
BUSH WD23 ....29 H3
Bushey Hall Golf Club
BUSH WD23 ....29 G1
Bushey Hall School
BUSH WD23 ....29 G3
Bushey Hall Swimming Pool
BUSH WD23 ....29 G2

Bushey Health Centre
BUSH WD23 ....29 G3
Bushey Heath Primary School
BUSH WD23 ....30 C5
Bushey Manor Junior School
BUSH WD23 ....29 G2
Bushey Meads School
BUSH WD23 ....30 B2
Bushey Museum & Art Gallery
BUSH WD23 ....29 H3
Byfleet Industrial Estate
WATW WD18 ....27 F5
Capital Business Centre
WATN WD24 ....11 E5
Cardiff Road Industrial Estate
WATW WD18 ....28 C3
Carpenders Park Cemetery
OXHEY WD19 ....35 G3
Central Primary School
WAT WD17 ....3 H4
Chater Infant School
WATW WD18 ....2 C5

Chater Junior School
WATW WD18 ....2 D5
Chenies Cricket Club
RKW/CH/CXG WD3 ....14 A3
Cherry Tree JMI School
WATN WD24 ....10 B5
Chorleywood Golf Club
RKW/CH/CXG WD3 ....24 C1
Chorleywood Health Centre
RKW/CH/CXG WD3 ....24 B1
Chorleywood Primary
RKW/CH/CXG WD3 ....24 B3
Christ Church CE
Primary School
RKW/CH/CXG WD3 ....25 E1
Coates Way Primary School
GSTN WD25 ....11 F2
Colnbrook School
OXHEY WD19 ....34 D1
Colne Bridge Retail Park
WAT WD17 ....3 K7
Colne Valley Retail Park
WAT WD17 ....3 K6

Colonial Business Park
WATN WD24........................ 18 D3

Community Mental
Health Centre
GSTN WD25........................ 10 D3

Cowley Hill Primary School
BORE WD6 .... 23 E3

CP House Business Centre
GSTN WD25........................ 19 G3

Delrow School
GSTN WD25........................ 20 B3

Discover Bible School
GSTN WD25........................ 10 D4

Divine Saviour RC
Primary School
ABLGY WD5......................... 9 G1

Eastbury Farm JMI School
NTHWD HA6 .... 34 A3

Edge Grove School
GSTN WD25........................ 20 B1

Elstree Aerodrome
BORE WD6 .... 21 E5

Elstree Golf Club
BORE WD6 .... 22 A5

Elstree Studios
BORE WD6 .... 22 D5

Elstree Way Clinic
BORE WD6 .... 23 E4

Fairbrook Medical Centre
BORE WD6 .... 23 E4

Fair Field Junior School
RAD WD7 .... 12 D5

Falconer School
BUSH WD23......................... 29 G2

Field Junior School
WATW WD18 .... 3 H6

Fisher Industrial Estate
WATW WD18 .... 3 G7

Francis Combe School
GSTN WD25........................ 10 D1

Frithwood Primary School
NTHWD HA6 .... 34 A5

Furzehill School
BORE WD6 .... 32 D1

Garston Clinic
WATN WD24........................ 10 C5

Garston JMI School
GSTN WD25........................ 11 E4

Garston Manor Special School
GSTN WD25........................ 10 D1

Garston Medical Centre
GSTN WD25........................ 10 D5

Gazelda Industrial Estate
WAT WD17 .... 3 J6

Greatham Road
Industrial Estate
BUSH WD23......................... 29 F1

Green End Business Centre
RKW/CH/CXG WD3 .... 15 F1

Greenfields Primary School
OXHEY WD19........................ 34 D4

Grimsdyke First &
Middle School
PIN HA5 .... 35 C5

Grims Dyke Golf Club
PIN HA5 .... 35 H3

Haberdashers' Aske's
Boys' School
BORE WD6 .... 21 C5

Haberdashers' Aske's
Girls' School
BORE WD6 .... 31 C1

Haberdashers RUFC
BORE WD6 .... 22 C4

Happy Valley Industrial Estate
KGLGY WD4 .... 5 E2

Harkness Industrial Estate
BORE WD6.......................... 32 D1

Harlequin Shopping Centre
WAT WD17 .... 3 G4

Hartspring Industrial Park
GSTN WD25........................ 19 H4

Hartspring Sports Centre
BUSH WD23......................... 19 H4

Harvey Road Primary School
RKW/CH/CXG WD3 .... 26 D3

Hertsmere Jewish
Primary School
RAD WD7 .... 21 H2

Highwood Primary School
BUSH WD23......................... 19 F3

Hille Business Centre
WATN WD24........................ 18 C3

Hill Farm Industrial Estate
GSTN WD25........................ 10 A2

Hillside School
BORE WD6 .... 33 F1

Holly Industrial Park
WATN WD24........................ 18 D3

Holmshill School
BORE WD6 .... 23 F4

Holy Rood Junior School
WAT WD17 .... 9 G5

Holy Rood RC Infant School
WAT WD17 .... 9 G5

Holywell School
WATW WD18 .... 28 A3

Home Park Industrial Estate
KGLGY WD4 .... 5 E4

Immanuel College
BUSH WD23......................... 30 D4

International University
BUSH WD23......................... 29 G1

Kenilworth First School
BORE WD6 .... 23 G5

Kinetic Business Centre
BORE WD6 .... 22 C5

Kings Langley Primary School
KGLGY WD4 .... 4 C2

Kings Park Industrial Estate
KGLGY WD4 .... 5 E3

Kingsway Infant School
GSTN WD25........................ 10 B3

Knutsford J & I School
WATN WD24........................ 19 E2

Laharna Trading Estate
WATN WD24........................ 18 D2

Laings Sports Ground
BAR EN5........................... 33 H1

Laurence Haines School
WATW WD18 .... 28 B3

Lea Farm Junior School
GSTN WD25........................ 11 E5

Leavesden Green Junior
Middle & Infant School
GSTN WD25........................ 10 B3

Leavesden Hospital
ABLGY WD5......................... 6 B5

Lismarrine Industrial Park
BORE WD6 .... 31 G3

Little Furze School
OXHEY WD19........................ 34 C2

Little Green Junior School
RKW/CH/CXG WD3 .... 16 D5

Little Reddings Primary School
BUSH WD23......................... 30 A2

Little St Helens School
NTHWD HA6 .... 34 A5

Lodge Sun Sports Club
WAT WD17 .... 17 H3

Lyndhurst Middle School
BORE WD6 .... 22 C3

Malvern Way Infant School
RKW/CH/CXG WD3 .... 27 F2

Manor Place Industrial Estate
BORE WD6 .... 23 F5

Meadow Wood School
BUSH WD23......................... 30 B2

Merchant Taylors School
NTHWD HA6 .... 27 H5

Meriden Primary School
GSTN WD25........................ 11 E5

Merryfield Primary School
BORE WD6 .... 22 C3

Monksmead School
BORE WD6 .... 23 F5

Moor Park Industrial Estate
NTHWD HA6 .... 27 F4

Mount Pleasant J & I School
LCOL/BKTW AL2 .... 7 F4

Mowat Industrial Estate
WATN WD24........................ 18 D2

Nascot Wood Junior School
WAT WD17 .... 18 B2

Nicholas Hawksmoor School
BORE WD6 .... 23 E3

North Watford Cemetery
GSTN WD25........................ 10 B4

North Watford Health Clinic
GSTN WD25........................ 10 D3

Oaklands College
BORE WD6 .... 23 F4

Odhams Industrial Estate
WATN WD24........................ 18 D1

Odhams Trading Estate
WATN WD24........................ 10 D5
WATN WD24........................ 10 B5

Old Merchant Taylors
Sports Club
RKW/CH/CXG WD3 .... 27 E1

Orchard Primary School
WATN WD24........................ 10 A5

Oxhey Infant School
BUSH WD23......................... 29 F3

Oxhey Wood Primary School
OXHEY WD19........................ 34 D3

Palace Theatre
WAT WD17 .... 3 F3

Paramount Industrial Estate
WATN WD24........................ 18 D2

Park Avenue Clinic
WAT WD17 .... 2 D1

Parkgate Infant School
WATN WD24........................ 18 D1

Parkgate Junior School
WATN WD24........................ 18 D1

Parkside Primary School
BORE WD6 .... 22 C2

Parmiters School
GSTN WD25........................ 6 D5

Peerglow Industrial Estate
WATW WD18 .... 27 E4

Pinner Hill Golf Club
PIN HA5 .... 34 C5

Porters Park Golf Club
RAD WD7 .... 13 H3

Public Swimming Pool
OXHEY WD19........................ 35 F4

Pump House Theatre
WAT WD17 .... 3 J6

The Purcell School
BUSH WD23......................... 19 G4

Queens School
BUSH WD23......................... 19 G5

Radlett Cricket Club
RAD WD7 .... 21 G1

Radlett Infant School
RAD WD7 .... 13 G5

Radlett Lodge School
RAD WD7 .... 13 G1

Radlett Preparatory School
RAD WD7 .... 21 H2

Rickmansworth School
RKW/CH/CXG WD3 .... 26 C3

Rickmansworth Sports Club
RKW/CH/CXG WD3 .... 26 B3

Rosary Priory High School
BUSH WD23......................... 30 D3

The Royal Masonic
School for Girls
RKW/CH/CXG WD3 .... 26 A2

Royal National
Orthopaedic Hospital
STAN HA7.......................... 31 G5

Rudolf Steiner School
KGLGY WD4 .... 4 B3

The Russell School
RKW/CH/CXG WD3 .... 24 A1

Ryde College
WATW WD18 .... 27 H3

Sacred Heart Junior
Middle & Infant School
OXHEY WD19........................ 29 G3

Saffron Green Primary School
BORE WD6 .... 33 H1

St Anthonys RC Junior School
WATW WD18 .... 27 H2

St Catherine of Sienna RC
Primary School
GSTN WD25........................ 11 E1

St Clement Danes School
RKW/CH/CXG WD3 .... 14 C4

St Hildas School
BUSH WD23......................... 30 A4

St Joan of Arc RC School
RKW/CH/CXG WD3 .... 26 B4

St Johns Infant School
RAD WD7 .... 13 E4

St Johns RC Primary School
RKW/CH/CXG WD3 .... 25 G5

St Johns School
NTHWD HA6 .... 34 C5

St Josephs RC School
OXHEY WD19........................ 34 C2

St Margarets School
BUSH WD23......................... 29 H4

St Meryl Junior Middle &
Infant School
OXHEY WD19........................ 35 F2

St Michaels RC School
GSTN WD25........................ 11 E1

St Nicholas School
BORE WD6 .... 32 B3

St Pauls CE Primary School
KGLGY WD4 .... 9 E3

St Peters Junior Middle &
Infant School
RKW/CH/CXG WD3 2

St Teresa's RC Primary School
BORE WD6.......................... 2

Sandown Road Industrial Estate
WATN WD24........................ 1

Shakespeare Industrial Estate
WATN WD24........................ 1

Sheepcot Medical Centre
GSTN WD25........................ 1

Shepherd Primary School
RKW/CH/CXG WD3 2

Skidmore Clinic
RKW/CH/CXG WD3 2

Stanborough School
GSTN WD25........................ 1

Stirling Industrial Centre
BORE WD6.......................... 1

Summerswood Primary School
BORE WD6.......................... 3

Sunderland Estate
KGLGY WD4 ....

Tabard RFC
RAD WD7 2

Tanners Wood Primary School
ABLGY WD5.........................

University of Hertfordshire
GSTN WD25........................ 1

Vale Industrial Estate
WATW WD18 2

Vicarage Road Cemetery
WATW WD18 ....

Warner Village Cinema
GSTN WD25........................

Warren Dell Primary School
OXHEY WD19........................ 3

Watersmeet Centre
RKW/CH/CXG WD3 ....

Waterways Heritage Museum
RKW/CH/CXG WD3 ....

Watford Arches Retail Park
WAT WD17 ....

Watford Business Centre
WAT WD17 ....

Watford Central
Swimming Baths
WAT WD17 ....

Watford County Court
WAT WD17 ....

Watford FC & Saracens RFC
(Vicarage Road Stadium)
WATW WD18 ....

Watford General Hospital
WATW WD18 ....

Watford Grammar School
for Boys
WATW WD18 ....

Watford Grammar School
for Girls
WATW WD18 ....

Watford Museum
WAT WD17 ....

Watford Sports &
Leisure Centre
GSTN WD25........................

The Wenta Business Centre
WATN WD24........................

Westfield School
WATW WD18 ....

West Hertfordshire College
WAT WD17 ....
WAT WD17 ....

West Herts Business Centre
BORE WD6..........................

West Herts College
BUSH WD23.........................

West Herts Golf Club
RKW/CH/CXG WD3 ....

William Penn Leisure Centre
RKW/CH/CXG WD3 ....

Wolsey Business Park
WATW WD18 ....

Woodhall School
OXHEY WD19........................

Woodlands Primary School
BORE WD6..........................

Woodside Stadium
GSTN WD25........................

York House School
RKW/CH/CXG WD3 ....